WASHINGTON AND THE MARROW RAIDERS

Susan hurried home f… ex… d ac… Bu… Gr… so… aft… run… pre…

And there was Aunt Barbara's finest creation – Washington – with red hair and freckles like Nicky Potts, the same gap between his teeth as Roy Sproggett. In fact he looked like *all* the boys in Castle Brading put together – the perfect Robot, until the Random Mischief Factor clicked into action.

Susan thought the next few weeks would be unusually exciting, and she was absolutely right as she, the marrows, Washington, the sinister Dr Delabole and practically everybody else in the village became mixed up in a thrilling and mysterious adventure.

Another fast-paced and funny novel from the talented author of *A Dinosaur called Minerva*.

Washington and the Marrow Raiders

Tessa Krailing

Illustrated by Hilda Offen

Hippo Books
Scholastic Publications Ltd
London

Scholastic Publications Ltd,
141-143 Drury Lane, London, WC2B 5TG England

Scholastic Book Services,
50 West 44th Street, New York 10036 NY USA

Scholastic Tab Publications Ltd,
123 Newkirk Road, Richmond Hill, Ontario L4C 3G5 Canada

H J Ashton Co Pty Ltd,
Box 579, Gosford, New South Wales, Australia

H J Ashton Co Pty Ltd,
9-11 Fairfax Avenue. Penrose, Auckland, New Zealand

First published by Scholastic Publications Ltd 1981

Made and printed in the USA
Typeset by Input Typesetting Ltd, London SW19 8DR
Set in Baskerville

WASHINGTON AND THE MARROW RAIDERS

For Dianne and Stanley Doubtfire

Chapter One
Poor Child!

The bell announced the end of afternoon school. Susan pushed her books into the desk and was first to reach the classroom door but Miss Delabole's voice rang out loud and clear. "Susan! You're window monitor this week, remember?"

Susan groaned – quietly, of course, so that Miss Delabole would not hear. She had forgotten she must stay behind to make sure all the windows and ventilators were properly closed. And today of all days, when she was so desperate to get home quickly!

There were ten windows in the classroom, five on each side. When they were all firmly shut Susan said, "May I go now, Miss Delabole?"

Miss Delabole looked up from the pile of books she was marking, a smile on her smooth white face. "Thank you, Susan. Why are you in such a hurry to get home today?"

"No special reason, Miss Delabole." She began to edge towards the door.

"I hope your grandfather is well?"

"Yes, thank you."

"And your great aunt?"

"Yes, thank you."

Susan did not like Miss Delabole. She was never exactly unkind but there was something cold and secret about her. She smiled a lot but never with her eyes, which were yellow and unblinking, like an owl's. Her hair hung in a straight black curtain with a fringe in front and her fingernails were painted green. Susan went on backing away to the door.

"Such an interesting person, your great aunt," Miss Delabole went on. "Has she produced any new inventions lately?"

"Not lately," said Susan, crossing her fingers behind her back. "Goodbye, Miss Delabole."

"Goodbye, Susan," said Miss Delabole, thoughtfully chewing the top of her red marking pen.

Susan hurried through the door, almost knocking over the Headmaster who was just about to enter. "Hey, steady on!" he warned, frowning. But when he looked down at her round, serious face his frown disappeared and he patted her kindly on the head. "Well, Susan Ramage, did you enjoy your summer holiday?"

"Yes, thank you, Sir."

"Stayed at home with your grandfather, I suppose?"

"Yes, Sir."

He gave an understanding nod. "Off you go, then."

When she had fled down the corridor he turned into the classroom, saying sadly under his breath, "Poor child. Poor child."

Susan weaved her way through the late afternoon shoppers in Castle Brading High Street and turned the corner into Chestnut Avenue. Her heart sank when she saw the Misses Trim walking towards her. Another delay! But she managed to smile as they came nearer.

"Hello, Susan," said Miss Evangeline Trim, tall and thin as a knitting needle. "Is school finished for today?"

"School finished?" asked Miss Lavinia Trim, short and dumpy as a pincushion, who always repeated what her sister said, only in a shortened form.

"Tell your grandfather we took his advice over our runner beans," said Miss Evangeline, "and it worked a treat."

"Worked a treat," echoed Miss Lavinia.

"Well, we mustn't keep you. Hurry on home to your tea." Miss Evangeline turned to watch Susan disappear down the road and murmured softly. "You know, Lavinia, I just can't help feeling sorry for that poor child."

"Poor child," agreed Miss Lavinia, nodding her head.

Chestnut Avenue led into Mulberry Road, where the Misses Trim lived, and Mulberry Road ran down the hill towards the river, ending up in Poplar Grove, which was a cul-de-sac. Susan opened the gate of No. 7 and ran down the side path. Here she stopped in surprise, confronted by a pile of sandbags barring her way. "Oh, not again!" she exclaimed and hurried round to bang on the front door. There was no reply so she lifted the letter-flap and called, "Grandad! It's only me."

She heard shuffling and grunting on the other side of the door as if furniture was being moved about. Then a voice said sternly, "What is your name?"

"Susan Ramage."

"State your business."

Susan sighed. "Please let me in, Grandad. It's Friday and I'm longing to see if Aunt Barbara's finished yet."

There came the sounds of bolts being drawn back, a chain lifted and a key turned in the lock. The door opened a crack and her grandfather's fierce face appeared, his moustache twitching suspiciously.

"It's all right, I'm quite alone," Susan assured him.

"Well, you can't be too careful." He opened the door wide enough to let her in, then shut it swiftly behind her, shooting the bolts across and sliding the chain back into position. "I found a footprint this morning on the marrow bed."

Susan hung her coat on the hook. "Did you, Grandad?"

"And another by the wall. I shall have to put up some wire netting. You'd think that wall would be high enough to stop anyone getting over, wouldn't you? But no!"

Susan murmured, "How awful," and changed her

outdoor shoes for a pair of comfortable moccasins.

"You know what it means, don't you?"

She shook her head.

"It means *someone*'s interested in my prize marrow. Wants to find out what the competition is before the Show. Hey, where d'you think you're going, young lady?"

"Upstairs to see Aunt Barbara."

"Give us a hand moving this stuff back against the door first."

Together they slid the table into position and piled up chairs and stools on top to make a barricade.

"I don't see what good it will do anyone, just finding out about your prize marrow," said Susan. "I mean, they've got to produce an even bigger one, haven't they?"

"Exactly! And if they can't do that you know what the next step is, don't you? Sabotage! But I'm ready for 'em." Grandad Ramage looked at the barricade with satisfaction. "No-one can get into the garden through the house, that's for sure. Nor round the side entrance – "

"They could always come by river," Susan reminded him, "and climb over the wall."

He gave a short laugh. "I'd like to see 'em try! There's booby traps all along the bank, every bit of it. I'll show you if you like."

"Later, Grandad. I must go and see Aunt Barbara first."

"Her and her explosions," he grumbled. "Bang, crash all day long. Still, at least it keeps the pigeons off me marrows."

Susan ran up three flights of stairs to find her Great Aunt Barbara.

Chapter Two

The Washington Formula

Now, although the Headmaster and the Misses Trim felt sorry for her, Susan herself thought she must be the luckiest person in the world to be living with Dame Barbara Blanchflower, the celebrated inventor. Here, in her laboratory on the attic floor of No. 7, Poplar Grove, Dame Barbara had invented the Whooshomatic, without which no kitchen is complete, and the Boomsprocket, a unique form of transport powered solely by garden compost. And here, for the past seventeen months, she had been hard at work on the most revolutionary, most technically advanced and above all most secret invention of her career.

And today – Friday, September 14 – was the day it was due to be completed at last!

Susan stood outside the laboratory, almost too nervous to knock. She could not hear a sound, none of the strange bubblings and burstings that usually came from within. It *must* be finished! She pressed a button that immediately identified her fingerprints and the door slid back.

She peered inside. The laboratory was in a state of total chaos, but that was nothing out of the ordinary. People often asked Dame Barbara how she managed to work in such a muddle, but she would reply that chaos was a necessary part of invention; you cannot create anything in a vacuum. So the shelves were piled high with glass tubes and twisted pipes and jars containing powders and crystals and liquids, while the floor space was filled with computer banks and filing cabinets and cooking stoves and video machines as well as a divan bed on which sat an enormous orange Persian cat called Moffatt. But Susan's eyes travelled quickly over these familiar objects, searching for something else. To her disappointment she could see nothing revolutionary or technically advanced or top secret at all.

"It's Friday, Aunt Barbara. You promised it would be finished by Friday," she said reproachfully.

Dame Barbara, wearing a royal blue tracksuit, was standing on her head in the corner. She sighed, which isn't easy when you're upside down, and said, "Yes Susan – it's Friday. And what am I doing at this precise moment, may I ask?"

Susan said doubtfully," Your Yoga exercises, I suppose." Then she realized what Dame Barbara meant. "Oh! You only allow yourself to relax completely after a major achievement. So you *have* finished!"

Dame Barbara carefully lowered her legs to the ground and stood upright, taking deep breaths. "Quite so." She began jogging up and down on the spot. As she was rather a large person this made the floorboards bounce alarmingly.

"Then – where is it?" Susan began to jog up and down as well from sheer excitement.

"Broom cupboard," said Dame Barbara shortly, touching her toes.

"May I look?"

"Go ahead."

Aware that this was an important moment, Susan opened the door of the broom cupboard very, very slowly. "Golly!" she exclaimed at last. "It's incredibly life-like."

Dame Barbara came to stand beside her, looking pleased. "So it jolly well should be. I took photographs of every boy in Castle Brading and made wax reproductions of at least half of them. It's got Nicky Potts' carrotty hair and freckles . . ."

"And Andy Weatherspoon's sticky-out ears!"

Dame Barbara nodded. "It's also got Roy Sproggett's gap between his two front teeth, only you can't see that until it smiles."

Susan stared at her. "You mean, it actually *smiles?*"

"Of course. Once it's switched on it looks and behaves exactly like a real boy. I defy anyone to tell the difference."

Susan peered closely into the broom cupboard. "I don't recognise the eyes," she said, "although there's *some*thing familiar about them."

"The eyes *are* a little unusual," Dame Barbara admitted. "But then we human beings have such limited vision. Moffatt, on the other hand, has excellent eyesight."

"So you copied Moffatt's eyes?" Susan looked at the cat. His amber eyes gazed unblinkingly back at her, bright as searchlights. She glanced again at Dame Barbara's invention. "Does that mean it can see in the dark?"

"Naturally."

"The only thing I don't understand," said Susan, looking puzzled, "is what people are going to use it *for.*"

Dame Barbara shrugged. "Jobs around the house or in the garden. Old ladies can send it out to do their shopping. It has an excellent memory."

"And does it do exactly what you tell it to do?"

"Ah!" said Dame Barbara. "Now that was something of a problem. Most boys *don't* do exactly what you tell them to do, so how life-like should I make it? I don't mind admitting, Susan, this invention gave me a good many headaches before I was finally satisfied."

"I'm not surprised," said Susan sympathetically. "It must have been terribly difficult to get it just right."

"Believe it or not, this is Mark III." Dame Barbara fished for her spectacles, which were suspended from a chain around her neck, and put them on to stare critically at her invention. "Mark I had a perfectly acceptable IPB – "

"That's an Individual Personality Base," said Susan, pleased with herself for remembering. "To make it look and sound different from anyone else."

"Right. But it didn't laugh at any of my jokes and I found that depressing, so I added SOH to the formula – a Sense of Humour. Mark II seemed quite perfect. In fact, that was the trouble. Very few boys, in my experience, are perfect. I had to think of something else and this time it was the RMF."

"What's the RMF?" asked Susan.

"The Random Mischief Factor. That means most of the time it will act logically, sensibly, reasonably. But every now and again the RMF will make it do something different, quite unexpectedly. In other words, it will behave in a much more realistic manner."

"So the formula is IPB plus SOH plus RMF . . . ?"

"That's it. But it must remain our secret, Susan." Dame Barbara looked serious. "If any unscrupulous person should get hold of that formula there's no knowing what he might do with it."

Susan nodded. "I promise I won't tell a soul. Not even Grandad. Though he's so absent-minded these days he'd never remember it anyway."

Dame Barbara chuckled. "Well, then – shall we make it work?"

"Yes, please. How do you switch it on?"

"Ah! To activate it you have to say its name."

"But I don't know its name."

Dame Barbara gazed at the portraits hanging on the wall above the bookcase. "There are, as you know, two men whom I admire above all others . . ."

"Do you mean you've named him after Uncle Stanley?" asked Susan. She glanced doubtfully at the stern face of Dame Barbara's husband, Dr. Stanley Blanchflower, who had set out to explore the remoter parts of the Andes five years ago, since when they had received from him only one picture postcard showing an aerial view of Lake Titicaca.

Dame Barbara shook her head and sighed deeply. "No, somehow I couldn't bring myself to call him Stanley. It would have sounded too much like a tribute to his memory." She straightened her shoulders bravely and gave Susan a bright smile. "So I've named him after the American president who could not tell a lie – "

Susan looked horrified. "You haven't called it *Washington*?"

"Indeed I have." Dame Barbara turned to point proudly at her invention. "And by saying his name you have now activated him. Look, Susan – Washington!"

Susan looked, and her mouth fell open with astonishment.

Rubbing his eyes, Washington yawned, stretched and stepped out of the broom cupboard. He smiled at Susan so that she could see the gap between his two front teeth and said, "I'm hungry. What's for tea?"

Chapter Three
A Birthday Party

"Ah, there you are," said Grandad Ramage crossly when Dame Barbara entered the kitchen. "That confounded machine of yours has gone wrong again."

Dame Barbara looked at her brother. "And is that all the welcome I get after being shut away in my laboratory for seventeen months? Not so much as a how-do-do or a nice-to-see-you-again-Barbara?" She walked over to the Whooshomatic and pressed the button marked COFFEE. The shute opened and whoosh! a mug came flying through the air straight into her waiting hands. She held the mug under the spout and a stream of dark liquid gushed into it, followed by a sugar lump and a plastic spoon. Dame Barbara sipped the coffee and said, "Excellent. Now what's wrong with that?"

"Humph!" Grandad Ramage glared at the Whooshomatic. "It may be all right on coffee, but I've been trying to cook some sausages for my tea for the last ten minutes and it keeps chucking 'em out as pink and flabby as when they went in."

"Oh, Grandad!" Susan had come into the kitchen with Washington close on her heels. "That's because you forgot to tell the machine whether you want them fried, grilled or toad-in-the-holed." She picked up a couple of sausages from the dish and put them into the machine, pressing the button marked GRILLED. Almost at once whoosh! they flew out of the shute, beautifully brown and done to a turn, landing neatly on the plate Susan was holding out for them.

Washington watched in fascination. "Hey, that's

good!" he exclaimed. "Can I have a go?"

"Certainly you may," said Dame Barbara. "In fact, you might as well cook enough for all of us. It seems a long time since I last had a square meal. Let's have some chips as well while we're about it." Looking about her she noticed for the first time that the kitchen was rather empty. "Where's the table, Arnold? And all the chairs . . . ?"

"In the hall," said Grandad Ramage shortly. "I've had to barricade the front door."

Dame Barbara showed no surprise. "We'll have to sit on the floor then, I suppose. Better get out a cloth, Susan."

Susan took a checked table cloth from a drawer and spread it out in the middle of the floor. Then she opened the cupboard and showed Washington the sack of potatoes. "Here you are," she said. "Put some into the Whooshomatic and don't forget to push the buttons for PEEL, CHIP and FRY."

Washington did exactly as Susan told him, standing ready with a dish to catch the shower of golden chips as they came out of the shute.

Grandad Ramage watched him with a puzzled expression. After a while he turned to Dame Barbara and asked, "Who's that? Friend of Susan's, I suppose." He scratched his head. "But how the devil did he get in?"

Dame Barbara smiled. "That, Arnold, is the result of seventeen months' hard work. What do you think of him?"

He stared hard at Washington. "But he's breathing! How can he breathe if he's only a – "

"Don't you dare say that word!" Dame Barbara banged her mug down fiercely. "My goodness, Washington is far superior to those ridiculous tin boxes on legs! Not only does he have lungs but also a simulated heart pumping warm liquid through a network of blue plastic tubes. It took me seven months to achieve the exact texture of flesh for the outer skin. What's more, he has a fully operational digestive system and an excellent appetite."

"These chips are smashing," said Washington, helping himself to a couple from the dish.

Susan knelt down on the floor and began setting out the knives and forks. "Let's make it a party," she said. "It can be Washington's birthday party."

"Good idea," agreed Dame Barbara. "We'll have a little celebration. Put some eggs, flour and icing sugar into the Whooshomatic, Susan, and push the button marked BIRTHDAY CAKE."

"A birthday cake!" Susan's eyes were shining. "With candles on it?"

"If you like, although strictly speaking he's not even a week old yet. Let's make it ten candles. That's a good round number."

Susan pushed all the buttons and held out a piece of round silver cardboard to catch the birthday cake. Whoosh! it came out already decorated with white icing, ten coloured candles and pink lettering which said, HAPPY BIRTHDAY, WASHINGTON.

"That's all very well," said Grandad Ramage, tucking his napkin under his chin, "but what *use* is he going to be, that's what I'd like to know? What can he *do*, apart from eat us out of house and home?"

"Oh, we'll find something, I've no doubt." Dame Barbara glanced at Washington, who was smothering his chips in tomato ketchup. "He can help Susan do the housework and give you a hand in the garden, for a start."

"In the garden?" Grandad Ramage sounded shocked. "I don't suppose he knows a weed from a hollyhock!"

Dame Barbara gave him a withering look. "Filed in his brain cells, may I inform you, is a vast store of computerised knowledge. Washington, tell us what you know about hollyhocks."

With the half-empty ketchup bottle poised above his plate Washington recited, "A garden perennial, originally a native of Asia, the hollyhock was introduced into the British Isles some three centuries ago. The flower spikes are three metres high and the – "

"Yes, that's all very interesting," interrupted Grandad Ramage impatiently, "but there's some things you can't learn from computers – and gardening's one of them."

"That's true enough." Dame Barbara regarded him with some concern. "You're looking tired, Arnold. I hope you haven't been overdoing things while I was busy upstairs?"

Susan said, "It's the Castle Brading Flower Show tomorrow week and Grandad has a very good chance of winning with his marrows again, only he thinks someone is trying to get into the garden and ruin them before the Show."

"What nonsense," said Dame Barbara. "Who on earth would want to do such a thing?"

Grandad Ramage choked with indignation. "There's plenty of folk jealous of my marrows, I can tell you! It could be any one of a dozen people."

"So he's been sitting up every night guarding them," Susan explained. "With a pitchfork in one hand and a bag of flour in the other."

"No wonder you're looking tired, Arnold." Suddenly Dame Barbara thumped the floor with her fist, making them all jump – all except Washington, that is, who was busy helping himself to some more chips. "There you are, then!" she exclaimed, looking pleased. "Tonight we'll set Washington to watch the marrows and you can have a good night's sleep."

Grandad Ramage said doubtfully, "He wouldn't know what to do – "

"He'll manage a good deal better than you with your little bag of flour," said Dame Barbara scornfully. "You want to find out who these villains are, don't you?"

"Well, yes . . . "

"Then leave it to me – and Washington."

Chapter Four

Night Watch

It was a dark night with hardly any moon. Now and again the clouds parted and a thin shaft of light illumined the garden, picking out Washington where he sat beside the marrow bed. Then it all went black again.

"Poor Washington," said Susan, looking down from a window in the laboratory. "I hope he's not afraid of the dark."

"He doesn't know what fear is," said Dame Barbara, who was standing behind her with a pair of infra-red field glasses trained on the scene below. "You must remember, Susan, that he's not capable of our human emotions – and a good thing, too, if you ask me. Think of all the trouble we have with them. Washington will never know what it's like to feel afraid or angry or sad – "

"But if he never feels sad he can never feel happy either," Susan pointed out. "And if he isn't afraid how can he avoid danger?"

"Ah well, I've built in certain safety factors to take care of any normal hazards he's likely to meet," said Dame Barbara. "As for happiness, he enjoys his food – his appetite makes sure of that. You mustn't expect too much of him, Susan."

"No," said Susan, with a sigh. "It's just that he's so very lifelike it's hard to remember he's not a real boy."

Grandad Ramage appeared in the doorway. "Anything happened yet?"

"Not yet. I do wish you'd go to bed, Arnold. You're

supposed to be having an early night."

"I can't sleep," he grumbled, coming to look out of the window. "Hey! Isn't that something floating down the river?"

Dame Barbara and Susan peered into the darkness. From their vantage point on the top floor they could just see the river as a faint ribbon of light when the moon came out and sure enough there seemed to be something moving steadily downstream, a long shadow gliding through the reeds.

"They've gone out of sight behind the wall," said Dame Barbara, lowering the field-glasses. "Two men in a rowing-boat – and it looked as if they were making ready to land on the towpath."

"Ha!" said Grandad Ramage with satisfaction. "That means they'll fall into my booby-traps. They won't get much farther."

"Even so I think we'll take no chances." Dame Barbara leaned out of the window and whispered, "Stand by, Washington. Remember what I told you – don't shoot until you have them clearly in your sights."

Washington waved to acknowledge her instructions and sat quite still, his bright amber eyes fixed on the garden wall.

"Any minute now you'll see a rocket go up," said Grandad Ramage. "Then the floodlights come on and a brass band plays 'Land of Hope and Glory' on the tape recorder."

They waited. For about two minutes nothing happened at all. Susan screwed her handkerchief into a ball, Dame Barbara tapped her foot impatiently on the floor and Grandad Ramage chewed his knuckles.

Then, quietly and stealthily, two dark shadows appeared on top of the wall.

"So much for your booby-traps, Arnold," muttered Dame Barbara. She leaned forward and hissed, "*Now*, Washington!"

A blinding flash lit up the figures on the wall, catching them just as they were about to leap into the garden. For a moment they remained transfixed, as if turned to stone, before falling backwards, one after the other, on to the towpath. Immediately the sky was flooded with light, a rocket zoomed heavenwards in a shower of coloured stars and "Land of Hope and Glory" rang out along the river bank.

"There you are! What did I tell you?" said Grandad Ramage gleefully.

"Oh, for goodness' sake, Arnold, go and turn that row off before the neighbours start complaining," Dame Barbara commanded. "All it's done is create a diversion so they can get clean away." She called out of the window. "Good boy, Washington. Bring the camera straight up here."

Grandad Ramage disappeared from the room and Susan turned to her great aunt. "It worked! He did exactly what you told him. Now we shall know who's been trying to get at Grandad's marrows."

"Of course!" Dame Barbara beamed. "Didn't I tell you how useful he could be?" She trained her glasses on the river again. "Just as I thought. There they go, rowing upstream as hard as they can."

At this point the noise outside ceased and the lights were turned off. "Poor Arnold," sighed Dame Barbara. "Somehow his little schemes never quite work out according to plan. I do wish he'd stick to gardening and leave the inventions to me."

"From now on he can," said Susan. "Washington will keep away intruders and Grandad can get on with preparing for the Show."

Washington entered the laboratory, waving the camera. "Did you see me take their photograph?" he asked proudly. "Wasn't I brilliant? I must be the greatest marrow-watcher in the world!"

"That's quite enough, Washington," said Dame Barbara sternly. "It's a good thing to take a pride in one's work but not to boast about it afterwards. Please record that in your memory bank."

"Righto," said Washington.

Dame Barbara took the camera and peeled off the print, holding it out to dry. Susan looked over her shoulder, watching the images of two men become clear and sharp. "I don't recognise either of them," she said at last.

When Grandad Ramage came back into the room they showed him the photograph. He studied it closely and nodded.

"Do you know them, Grandad?" asked Susan.

"Aye, I do. The foxy-faced man is the gamekeeper up at the Castle. I've seen him having a pint sometimes at the 'Rose and Crown'. And the moon-faced one was handing round the sandwiches last week when Lady Brading invited the Horticultural Society to look round the Castle grounds. I think he's a footman or a butler or somesuch."

"So they both work for Lord Brading!" exclaimed Dame Barbara. "There's your answer then, Arnold. Lord Brading is your greatest rival in the vegetable class, isn't he? Well, now you know who's trying to ruin your chances."

Grandad Ramage turned pale. "Not Lord Brading! He wouldn't do a thing like that."

Dame Barbara handed him the photograph. "There's your proof."

He took it and left the room, still muttering to himself, "I just can't believe it. Always seemed such a nice chap . . ."

When the door had closed behind him Susan said, "Poor Grandad. I wonder what he'll do now."

"That's up to him." Dame Barbara yawned and glanced at her watch. "Time we were all in bed."

"What about Washington? Does he go to sleep?"

"Of course. That's when he recharges his batteries."

"But how do we switch him off?"

"Same way as you switch him on – by sound. All you have to say is BROOM CUPBOARD . . ." she paused and waited while Washington entered the broom cupboard and closed the door – "and he will continue to work until he's actually inside. It's one of the safety factors, you see. No matter where he is when you say the words he will always wait until he reaches the broom cupboard before switching himself off."

"Aunt Barbara, could I take him out tomorrow? Introduce him to some people and see if they notice anything unusual?"

"I don't see why not . . ."

"Oh, that would be marvellous!" Susan could hardly wait to try out Dame Barbara's invention on the unsuspecting people of Castle Brading.

Chapter Five

A Visit to the Supermarket

"Look who's here, Lavinia," said Miss Evangeline Trim, leading the way into the living-room where her sister was busy dusting china ornaments on the mantelshelf. "It's Susan Ramage come to see if we want anything at the shops and she's brought a little friend with her."

"Little friend?" Miss Lavinia looked up in surprise.

"His name's Washington," said Susan.

She watched their faces to see if they noticed anything unusual but they both beamed at Washington, who beamed obligingly back.

"And where do you live, Washington?" inquired Miss Evangeline.

Before he could open his mouth to say "broom cupboard" Susan answered quickly, "He's come to stay with us. Probably for good."

"For good?" Miss Lavinia's pale blue eyes were full of concern. "But what about his mummy and daddy?"

"He's an orphan," said Susan. "Like me."

Miss Evangeline gave her sister a quelling look and muttered under her breath, "Really, Lavinia, you can be so tactless at times! Can't you see this is splendid news? He'll be company for Susan."

Miss Lavinia blushed with shame and said hastily, "Yes, company for Susan. Splendid news."

"We came to see if you'd like us to do the shopping for you this morning," said Susan.

"Indeed we would," said Miss Evangeline. "Wait a minute while I make out a list . . ."

"Oh, there's no need to do that. If you tell Washington what you want he'll remember everything," said Susan.

"My goodness, what a clever boy!" Miss Evangeline gave Washington an admiring look. "Well, we could do with some washing powder . . ." She reeled off a long list of things they needed and Washington nodded after each item to show it was recorded in his memory. When she had finished he recited it all back to check that it was correct and they both stared at him in amazement. Then Miss Evangeline gave some money to Susan and Miss Lavinia fetched two shopping bags for them to take.

"Never heard anything like it," murmured Miss Evangeline as they stood on the doorstep to wave them off. "That boy's a genius, if you ask me."

"If you ask me that boy's a genius," agreed Miss Lavinia.

Castle Brading High Street was crowded with people doing their weekend shopping, but no-one gave Washington a second glance as he walked along beside Susan. He gazed about him with great interest, staring up into everyone's faces. "Isn't it strange?" he said at last. "There are so many people in the world and yet they all look different. I haven't seen anyone else at all like me."

"Neither have I," said Susan, thinking privately that although Dame Barbara had taken great trouble to make Washington extremely life-like there was nonetheless something a little odd about his appearance. Perhaps it was Moffatt's watchful yellow eyes combined with that shock of carrotty hair and freckles, but somehow he did not look quite like other boys.

"It's funny, I didn't know I was an orphan," he remarked, just as they arrived at the supermarket.

Susan stared at him. "But you're not. You're a – " She stopped herself in the nick of time. Oh, poor Washington! she thought; he doesn't realize he's a robot. Aunt Barbara must have forgotten to feed the knowledge into his computer. Quickly she changed the subject. "Goodness, here we are at the supermarket already. Now keep close to me, Washington, whatever you do. Aunt Barbara would never forgive me if I lost you."

As soon as they were inside the store Susan gave him the wire trolley to push and turned away to pick out a jar of coffee. When she looked round she saw Washington lying flat on his stomach on top of the trolley, giving himself a ride between the tinned fruit and the frozen meats.

"Oh dear," she exclaimed, hurrying after him. "Washington, that's meant for the shopping, not for you. Anyway, you're supposed to be telling me what's on the list."

For a while he followed her obediently while she collected the items Miss Evangeline had asked them to buy, but when they reached the biscuit section she took a long time deciding which particular brand of chocolate crunchies she should take and Washington grew bored. His eye fell on the enormous pyramid of baked beans which one of the assistants had just finished building and at that very moment the Random Mischief Factor Dame Barbara had implanted in his mechanism clicked into place.

"Baked beans," he said loudly, looking about him. "I think we ought to take one of these." And leaning down he selected a tin from the bottom of the pyramid.

There was a slow rumbling of metallic thunder as the pile came crashing down. Tins of baked beans rolled everywhere – up to the delicatessen counter, down to the checkout desks and under the shelves of herbs and spices. They scattered bottles of sauce like skittles and completely demolished a display of pet food. Some people laughed and some stood still in horrified silence. A few clicked their tongues disapprovingly.

When the last tin finally came to rest against the frozen fish counter the manager descended from his office above the store to survey the scene of destruction. His gaze travelled quickly over the other shoppers and arrived at Washington, who still held in his hand a single tin of baked beans. "I wonder," he said in a slow, deliberate voice, "if anyone is going to admit responsibility for this regrettable incident."

"Oh yes," said Washington without hesitation, truthful as his namesake. "It was me. I knocked them down."

There was a moment's silence. Everyone stared at Washington.

"I see," said the manager. "Perhaps you would care to come into my office, young man . . ."

Her heart sinking, Susan stepped forward to stand beside Washington, but before she could say a word a familiar voice rang out behind her. "No, Mr Peabody, the fault is entirely mine. The children are with me and I am responsible for them."

Susan turned in amazement to see Miss Delabole smiling at the manager, whose manner changed abruptly. "Why, Miss Delabole," he said in a quite different tone of voice. "I had no idea . . ."

"Susan and her friend are helping me," Miss Delabole continued, still smiling. "I'm afraid there was a little mishap with the baked beans but the pyramid was not awfully well built . . ." Her voice trailed away reproachfully.

Mr Peabody cleared his throat. "Ah well, accidents will happen and there's no use crying over spilt – er – beans. I trust you're keeping well, Miss Delabole? And your brother?"

"Very well, thank you." Miss Delabole put one hand on Susan's shoulder and the other on Washington's and propelled them towards the checkout desk. "You'll forgive me if we hurry on? So much to do, you know."

"Of course." Mr Peabody watched them join the queue of shoppers waiting to pay and then turned to the nearest assistant. "Pick up the tins and rebuild the display," he commanded. "And make sure you do the job properly this time!"

Once they were safely outside the store Susan said

uncomfortably, "Thank you very much for helping us, Miss Delabole. I'm afraid it was really Washington's fault."

"I know," smiled Miss Delabole. "I'd been watching you both for some time." Her eyes rested thoughtfully on Washington. "Aren't you going to introduce me to your friend?"

Hastily Susan made the introductions and then seized Washington firmly by the arm. "We ought to take the shopping straight back to the Misses Trim now. Thank you again, Miss Delabole."

"That's all right, Susan. I'll see you on Monday. And how about Washington? Will he be coming to school with you?"

"I – I'm not sure."

"Do bring him if you can. Goodbye for now."

Miss Delabole watched them hurrying up the High Street. When they were out of sight she turned into the car park where her brother was waiting in a long, low Ferrari. "I was right," she said quietly as she slid into the passenger seat. "Dame Barbara has excelled herself this time. It's a magnificent piece of work, totally lifelike and even warm to the touch."

"Be quiet!" Dr Lucius Delabole's sharp black beard quivered with fury. "That infernal woman! Must she always better me at every turn?" He glared at his sister. "I want to see it for myself, Hermione. Can you bring it to me?"

"I'll do my best," said Miss Delabole soothingly. "I'll certainly do my best."

Chapter Six
The Boomsprocket

As soon as Susan and Washington had delivered the shopping to the Misses Trim and received a chocolate bar each for their trouble they went straight home to Poplar Grove. Here they found Dame Barbara in the garage, polishing the Boomsprocket.

She straightened up as they appeared and asked, "Well? How did you get on?"

Susan told her. When she reached the part about the baked beans Dame Barbara laughed till the tears ran down her cheeks. "It wasn't really all that funny at the time," Susan pointed out. "I don't know what made him do it."

"I do," said Dame Barbara, still chuckling. "The good old RMF, that's what it was."

"Well, at least he owned up,"

"Of course he owned up! Like his namesake he cannot tell a lie." Dame Barbara patted Washington affectionately on the head. "Good boy. You did very well."

"All the same, I can't think what would have happened if Miss Delabole hadn't appeared," said Susan, frowning. "I wonder why she decided to help us. It seems rather peculiar."

"Just a kindly deed, I expect. After all, you are in her class at school."

Susan lowered her voice. "Aunt Barbara, can I have a word with you in private?"

"Yes, of course. Hang on a minute." Dame Barbara propelled Washington towards the back of the garage, where Grandad Ramage was busy filling the Boom-

sprocket's fuel tanks with compost. "Arnold? Here's Washington to give you a hand."

"About time too," muttered her brother, up to his elbows in leaf mould.

Dame Barbara took Susan aside. "Now what is it? Did something else go wrong – something you haven't told me about?"

"Not exactly, but I think there's a vital piece of information you've forgotten to feed into Washington's computer. The trouble is, he doesn't seem to know he's a robot."

"Oh, is that all?" Dame Barbara's face cleared. "We can fix that soon enough. In fact, I'll tell him now, though I must admit I find the term 'robot' quite inappropriate for something as technically advanced as Washington . . ."

"No, please don't tell him," Susan said quickly. "You might hurt his feelings."

Dame Barbara sighed. "Susan, how often do I have to remind you that Washington doesn't have any feelings?"

"I think he does," said Susan obstinately. "And anyway, surely it's safer if he doesn't know? Then he won't give himself away if anyone asks him. You said he can't tell a lie . . ."

"By heaven, that's good thinking, Susan!" Dame Barbara gave a hearty laugh of approval. "You're right – it's far better he doesn't know." She turned to her brother. "Have you finished yet, Arnold? We ought to be on our way if we're going."

"Are you taking the Boomsprocket out for a drive?" asked Susan.

Dame Barbara nodded. "We thought we'd pop up to the Castle to show Lord Brading the photograph and see what he has to say about it. Do you want to come too?"

"Yes, please!" Washington immediately leapt straight in and settled himself on the canvas seat.

"But there's only room for three of us," Susan said doubtfully.

"That's all right. Your grandfather can drive and

I'll run along behind," said Dame Barbara. "The exercise will do me good. Buck up, Arnold! We must have enough compost in by now to get us to Scotland and back."

Grandad Ramage put aside his spade and clambered in, muttering under his breath. He pushed the starter button and the engine spluttered into life, settling down into a steady chug-chug as it rolled slowly out of the garage and down the drive.

The Boomsprocket looked rather like a wheelbarrow perched on a pair of garden rollers with a motor-mower at the back. It was a colourful sight as it thundered down Poplar Grove, the red-and-white striped awning flapping in the breeze. If people fled into their houses at its approach and rushed to fasten their doors and windows it was not so much to shut out the noise (it sounded like a dozen full-sized steam-rollers) as the *smell*, especially when it backfired, which it did fairly frequently. But if ever Dame Barbara received any complaints she always replied that it came from good healthy organic matter, far less likely to pollute the atmosphere than noxious petrol fumes.

The Boomsprocket rumbled steadily up Mulberry Road and turned left into Willow Walk alongside the river, with Dame Barbara keeping up a rhythmic trot several metres behind.

At the end of Willow Walk they came to the Castle gates, which stood open, and proceeded up the drive, finally rolling to a halt beside some stone steps leading up to the great oak doors.

As Grandad Ramage climbed down from the driver's seat Dame Barbara arrived, slightly out of breath. "What's going on, Arnold? Where is everybody?"

Now that the engine had spluttered into silence the Castle seemed uncannily quiet. All the windows were closed and nothing stirred except the leaves on the trees. "Go and ring the bell, Washington," said Dame Barbara.

Washington jumped down and ran up the steps to tug at the heavy iron ring hanging down beside the door. Nothing happened. He waited for a while, then pulled it again.

This time the door opened to reveal Lord Brading's butler, sloppily dressed in his shirtsleeves and carpet slippers. "Yes?" He did not sound particularly welcoming.

"Good morning," said Washington politely. "Would you please tell Lord Brading that Dame Barbara Blanchflower and Mr Arnold Ramage have come on important business. As well as Susan and me," he added.

"Push off!" growled the butler, eyeing the Boomsprocket with disgust. "And take that contraption with you."

"How dare you!" Dame Barbara came to stand at the foot of the steps with her arms folded and her eyes blazing. "Kindly inform Lord Brading immediately that we wish to see him."

The butler gave her an uncertain look. "He's not here. Gone on holiday. Won't be back till Friday."

"Aha!" Dame Barbara nodded her head wisely. "So that's the way of it. While the cat's away the mice do play! *Very* interesting."

"Stupid woman's round the bend," muttered the butler, and slammed the door.

"Come along, Washington," said Dame Barbara. "It's obvious we'll get no satisfaction here today."

"What a horrible man," said Susan. "But he wasn't the man in the photograph, was he? The one with the moon face, I mean, that Grandad said he'd seen handing round the sandwiches."

"True enough," Dame Barbara agreed. "Still, there's not much we can do now till Lord Brading returns next Friday. And that's only a day before the Show! We'll just have to keep a close watch on those marrows of yours, Arnold." She turned towards her brother, but he was nowhere to be seen. "Arnold? *Now* where's he's gone?"

"He went through a gate in the wall," said Susan. "I think he saw someone he knew."

Grandad Ramage had caught sight of the battered

tweed hat belonging to Nat Rumbold, Lord Brading's head gardener, who was pottering along behind the runner beans. "Hello, Nat," he called, casting a critical eye over the neat rows of healthy-looking vegetables. "Everything coming along well for next week, then?"

"Mustn't grumble," said Nat with a knowing grin. "How are your marrows, Arnold?"

"Well enough," replied Grandad Ramage cagily.

"I don't mind telling you his Lordship intends to beat you this year," said Nat. "He'll stop at nothing to bring home that Cup for his mantelshelf."

Grandad Ramage, on whose mantelshelf the Cup now rested, turned pale and produced the photograph from inside his coat. "Have a look at this, Nat. Ever seen these fellows before?"

Nat studied the photograph and nodded. "Of course. That's Gamekeeper Sharpe and young Gordon . . ." He stopped as if afraid he had said too much and added hastily, "But I could be mistaken. It's not very clear, is it? Looks as if you caught them by surprise. Where was this taken, Arnold?"

"Doesn't matter," mumbled Grandad Ramage, replacing the photograph inside his coat. "Well, mustn't keep you, Nat. See you next Saturday at the Show.

"You will, you will!" Nat Rumbold gave a gusty wheeze of laughter.

Grandad Ramage returned to the Boomsprocket and climbed into the driving seat. "I don't like it," he muttered as they chugged back down the river. "I don't like it one bit!"

Chapter Seven

An Invitation to Tea

"Where's Washington?" Susan asked when she went up to the laboratory on Sunday morning.

"In the broom cupboard, resting after his night's work," replied Dame Barbara.

"Did anything happen? I didn't hear a sound."

Dame Barbara shook her head. "Not a thing. Perhaps they've given up."

"Or maybe they're just planning their next move." Susan looked at her great aunt, who had exchanged her tracksuit for a knitted purple tunic. "Are you coming to church?"

"Of course." Dame Barbara moved Moffatt from the top of a hat box and took out an orange straw boater, which she decided would look particularly bright and cheerful with the purple. "I thought we'd take Washington."

"Will he behave himself?" asked Susan, thinking that the RMF could cause even more havoc in church than at the supermarket.

Dame Barbara shrugged. "I want to try out his vocal chords," she explained. "He's equipped with perfect pitch and programmed to respond to any keynote, but I'd like to put him through a practical test."

They drove to church in the Boomsprocket, leaving Grandad Ramage to mind his marrows. By the time they arrived the choir was already processing up the centre aisle, so they slipped into a pew at the back, behind the Misses Trim.

Washington stared at the choirboys. "Why aren't I dressed in a long white shirt with a frilly collar?"

he demanded in such a loud voice that both Dame Barbara and Susan turned to shush him fiercely.

But as soon as they began to sing the opening hymn Susan was first astonished and then delighted and finally proud to be standing next to Washington. His voice rang out clear and tuneful as a bell, soaring up to the top notes with ease. Several people looked round to see where this glorious sound was coming from and Dame Barbara wore a satisfied smile.

When the service was over they filed out into the churchyard where the Vicar was waiting to greet them. "How delightful to see you again, Dame Barbara, after all this time." He shook her warmly by the hand. "And what exciting new inventions have you been producing for us, I wonder?"

Dame Barbara chuckled. "Oh, I might have one or two little surprises up my sleeve. By the way, I don't think you've met young Washington, who's staying with us at present?"

While the Vicar was shaking hands with Washington Miss Evangeline Trim came up to them, her flowered hat trembling with emotion. "My dear Vicar," she began dramatically, "I must insist you recruit this young man for the choir immediately! Never in my life have I heard such a voice. He sings like an angel!"

"Like an angel," echoed Miss Lavinia from behind her sister.

Just at that moment the choirboys came hurtling out of the vestry door, now looking their usual untidy selves and fighting over a packet of biscuits provided by the Vicar's wife. When they saw the Vicar they fell into a sedate walk and Nicky Potts hung around to stare at Washington, whose carrotty hair and freckles exactly matched his own.

Dame Barbara said goodbye to the Vicar and had just turned to walk down the path when a gloved hand was laid on her arm. "Dame Barbara, I'm *so* glad to have caught you."

It was Miss Delabole, wearing a black silk suit and a round velvet hat with a black spotted veil.

Dame Barbara greeted her enthusiastically. "Miss Delabole, I understand we have *you* to thank for coming to the rescue of these two children yesterday."

"Really it was nothing," protested Miss Delabole. "I was only too glad to be able to help. After all, Susan *is* one of my best pupils."

Susan wriggled uncomfortably as Miss Delabole put an arm round her shoulder.

"And how about your little visitor?" Miss Delabole's gaze slid to Washington, who had fallen some way behind. "Shall you be sending him to school with Susan on Monday?"

Susan tugged warningly at her aunt's sleeve, but it was no use. Still flushed with triumph at the success of Washington's vocal chords Dame Barbara now had a vision of him dazzling the education authorities. "I don't see why not."

"Oh, splendid!" Miss Delabole's eyes gleamed through her veil. "We'll take great care of him – won't we, Susan?"

Although Susan thought this rather an odd thing to say she nodded, hoping that would be the end of the conversation, but Miss Delabole's manner became even more friendly. "You know, Dame Barbara, my brother Lucius is always saying how much he would like to meet you, since you're both in the same line of business, so to speak." When she saw Dame Barbara looking blank she explained, "He is Dr Lucius Delabole, the well-known scientist. No doubt you've seen him on television?"

Dame Barbara never had time to watch television but did not wish to appear rude, so she said vaguely, "Oh, yes . . ."

"He also does a little inventing in his spare time," Miss Delabole continued smoothly, "so I'm sure you'd have a great deal in common. Could you possibly come to tea this afternoon? And bring the children, of course."

"How kind," said Dame Barbara, "but . . ."

"That's settled then. We'll expect you at about four o'clock at 'The Briars'. Susan knows where it is –

don't you, dear?"

Susan nodded miserably. Tea with Miss Delabole and her horrible brother! Could anything be worse?

Miss Delabole bade them goodbye and disappeared as swiftly as if she had vanished into thin air.

"Odd woman," remarked Dame Barbara. "Still, I daresay it'll be interesting to meet this brother of hers. I'm always ready to offer a helping hand to the enthusiastic amateur. Where's Washington?"

They looked back to see him standing in the centre of a group of choirboys. When Dame Barbara called he came at once and climbed into the Boomsprocket.

"Those boys," he told them, "put out their tongues at me."

"So what did *you* do?" inquired Dame Barbara.

"Put out my tongue at them, of course. Then one of them pinched my arm so I pinched him back. And another kicked my leg so I stamped on his foot."

"I'm afraid boys are like that, Washington," said Susan. "If you come to school with me you'll find a lot of pinching and kicking and stamping goes on every playtime."

"Oh, good!" said Washington.

Chapter Eight

Encounter on the Towpath

As it was such a fine autumn morning Miss Delabole decided to walk home from church beside the river. She was feeling particularly pleased with herself so she hummed a little tune as she turned into Willow Walk and opened the gate on to the towpath. How delighted Lucius would be with the news that Dame Barbara was bringing Washington to tea! It might even put him in a sweeter mood for the rest of the day.

But when she followed the towpath along behind the houses in Poplar Grove a curious sight met her eyes. Two men, one standing on the other's shoulders, appeared to be trying to see over the wall into someone's back garden. Miss Delabole counted along the gates. One, three, five, seven – yes, it was undoubtedly Dame Barbara's garden.

She slowed her pace and walked quietly towards them, but as she drew near she accidentally kicked a stone into the water, where it fell with a loud plop. Immediately the stout young man in a bowler hat tugged at the trouser leg of the red-haired man balancing on his shoulders and they both collapsed into a heap at Miss Delabole's feet.

"Good morning," she said brightly, as if she had noticed nothing unusual. "Lovely day, isn't it?"

"Aye, lovely day," growled the red-haired man, giving her a foxy grin. "Just the weather for a spot of birdwatchin'."

"Oh, is *that* what you were doing?" inquired Miss Delabole. "And did you see anything interesting?"

"Not a thing." The bowler-hatted man, his round face shiny with perspiration, sat up and rubbed his shoulder. "Trouble is, you see, the leaves have grown so big they completely cover the . . ."

"Shut your trap, Gordon!" snarled his companion, "and leave the talkin' up to me." As he got to his feet he gave Miss Delabole a reassuring smile, displaying pointed yellow teeth. "Oh yes, Ma'am. We've seen somethin' interestin' all right. A lesser-spotted marrow bird, that's what we've seen."

"Really?" said Miss Delabole. "I didn't know such a bird existed."

"Nor me," agreed Gordon.

The foxy-faced man cuffed him round the ear and then turned his yellow grin back to Miss Delabole. "But then it's very rare, you see. *Very* rare, the marrow bird."

"How fascinating." Miss Delabole raised her veil to give them both a closer look. "I'm sure we've met somewhere before. Haven't I see you up at the Castle?"

The foxy-faced man was about to deny it, but before he could say a word Gordon had replied eagerly, "Oh, yes, we works up at the Castle all right. Fancy you spottin' us. Must have a good memory for faces, mustn't she, Sep? Ow!" This last squeal of pain was caused by a savage thump in the back from his companion.

Miss Delabole smiled. "Yes, I have. Surely you're Septimus Sharpe, Lord Brading's gamekeeper?"

The foxy-faced man shuffled his feet and gave her a hard stare. "What if I am?" he demanded.

Miss Delabole turned the pearly brilliance of her smile on Gordon, who was so dazzled he whipped off his bowler hat and clutched it to his chest. "And I'm Gordon," he informed her, blushing a little. "Gordon Twist, second footman – doubling as third gardener when it's Nat Rumbold's day off."

"What an unusual combination," remarked Miss Delabole admiringly. "You must be very versatile."

"He is, he is!" Septimus Sharpe caught hold of his

friend's left ear and hauled him closer. "Turns his hand to all sorts of jobs, does Gordon, and makes a muck of every single one of 'em!"

"Oh, surely not," said Miss Delabole in a soothing voice. "You must both be very efficient, otherwise you'd not be in Lord Brading's employment."

Septimus Sharpe let go of Gordon's ear and they both regarded her blankly, not quite sure how to respond to this flattery. For a few moments they all stood in silence, each waiting for the other to move first, but since Miss Delabole's stare was by far the hardest, brightest and most powerful it was eventually the two men who began to shuffle backwards, towards the boat moored in the reeds.

"Goodbye," Miss Delabole called after them. "I hope we may meet again some time."

She watched them rowing hard up river until they disappeared round the bend and continued her way along the towpath towards The Drive, a wide avenue lined with beech trees leading up the hill to the select part of Castle Brading where she lived with her brother.

She found Dr Lucius Delabole in his observatory, peering through a telescope directed not at the sky but down the hill to No. 7, Poplar Grove. "Guess who's coming to tea!" she said triumphantly, and told him the good news.

He did not smile, but then he never smiled. Even so, she could tell he was pleased by the way his long fingers pulled at his pointed black beard.

Although unwilling to risk undoing the good she had already done, Miss Delabole felt bound to add, "However, I fear we may not be the only people interested in Dame Barbara's little experiment."

Her brother listened attentively as she related her encounter on the towpath. After a few moments his fingers stopped pulling at his beard and began drumming on the arm of his chair instead.

"But what I didn't discover," she concluded, "is whether they're working for themselves or Lord Brading."

Dr Delabole shook his head. "His Lordship does not possess a scientific mind."

"Neither, I would have said, do Septimus Sharpe or Gordon Twist," his sister pointed out. "Yet they were certainly interested in Dame Barbara's house."

"You may have been mistaken, Hermione. Perhaps they were only birdwatching after all."

"Have *you* ever heard of a marrow bird?"

He admitted he had not.

Miss Delabole stood up. "However, I am more than satisfied with the morning's work. But I do think, Lucius, you should lock the laboratory door before you show Dame Barbara round. We can always pretend you've mislaid the key. If she should catch sight of some of your recent work she would be immediately suspicious."

He nodded agreement and rubbed his hands until the knuckles cracked. "I must confess I'm looking forward to this afternoon's little – er, entertainment. I should certainly like to inspect the control panel. Is it located in the head, I wonder, or in the chest . . .?"

Miss Delabole smiled. "I've no idea, but doubtless you'll be able to discover that for yourself. Now I shall go and cut some cucumber sandwiches for tea. To my mind there's nothing like cucumber sandwiches for persuading people that all's well with the world."

Chapter Nine

Tea at "The Briars"

As the Boomsprocket rumbled up The Drive that afternoon Susan told her great aunt, "You can't miss the house. It's all white and streamlined, with portholes like an ocean liner. There it is!"

"No wonder it's called 'The Briars'," said Dame Barbara, noticing the high impenetrable forest of brambles surrounding the garden like a barbed-wire fence. "Where's the gate?"

"It's more of a portcullis, really," said Susan, "and it lifts automatically when you tell it who you are."

The Boomsprocket coughed to a halt outside a steel-mesh barrier, three metres high. "This is a recorded announcement," said the disembodied voice of Dr Lucius Delabole. "What is your name and the purpose of your visit? Speak NOW."

Dame Barbara stared at the barrier. Washington, who replied truthfully to all questions, announced their names loudly and clearly and said they had come to tea. Immediately the portcullis was raised and they were able to drive underneath.

"Ingenious," commented Dame Barbara as it crashed down behind them, "if a little primitive."

The Boomsprocket backfired twice when it reached the front door to proclaim their arrival, and the door was opened at once by Miss Delabole in a floating yellow afternoon gown. "How lovely to see you all! My brother is *delighted* you were able to come."

Inside, "The Briars" seemed enormous, far larger than it looked from the outside; but this was because many of the walls were lined with mirrors and the floor was made of black glass. Washington soon discovered it was fun to slide on and had to be restrained by Dame Barbara, whereas Susan twice apologised for bumping into someone as she turned a corner only to discover it was her own reflection.

"You must come and meet my brother straight away." Miss Delabole led them into a large room where the walls were white and the furniture black. The floor was covered with white furry carpet which Susan had a horrid suspicion might be made from polar bears, and they did not at first see Dr Delabole because his black-and-white kaftan merged so well with the background.

After they had exchanged a few pleasantries about the weather the conversation seemed to fizzle out, partly because Washington had by now discovered that the black leather sofa made an odd gasping sound when he bounced up and down on it. Miss Delabole said quickly, "Lucius, why don't you take Washington up to look at your observatory?"

"An observatory?" Dame Barbara leapt to her feet. "What rattling good fun. I adore telescopes! Tell me, do you specialise in lunar, stellar or solar observations?"

"Yes," said Dr Delabole vaguely.

He shot a furious look at his sister, but she merely gave a resigned shrug and said, "Well, in that case I'll go and get the tea while you take our visitors upstairs, Lucius."

Scowling, Dr Delabole stalked across the furry carpet, followed by Dame Barbara, Susan and Washington. In the centre of the hall was a lift cage. Dr Delabole pressed a button and immediately a stainless steel box descended from the floor above.

Washington looked pleased at the prospect of his first ride in a lift and even Dame Barbara seemed impressed. Susan, however, could not help feeling nervous at being shut inside such a small space with Dr Delabole, who was behaving rather oddly, staring at the back of Washington's head and even trying to peer into his left ear-hole.

The lift took them up two floors into a huge glass dome. Dame Barbara was first out of the lift and went straight to the powerful telescope. "What a splendid piece of equipment!" she exclaimed, peering into it.

While she was thus occupied Dr Delabole took the opportunity to subject Washington to a close scrutiny, and at one time patted him so hard on the back that he made him choke.

"Now this looks fascinating." Dame Barbara put on her spectacles to examine a working model of the solar system. "Can you explain it to us, Doctor? I'm sure the children would love to know how it works."

Dr Delabole reeled off a complicated description of the mechanism governing the movement of the planets, which Susan found impossible to follow. Washington, of course, already knew it all, so after a few minutes he moved away to look through the telescope.

"Dr Delabole, I have to congratulate you," said Dame Barbara. "It seems to me you're a man of many talents. I should very much like to see your laboratory if you can spare the time."

"Not possible," he said abruptly. "Experiment in progress. Mustn't disturb."

Dame Barbara nodded. "I quite understand. Been through it all myself."

Suddenly there was a high-pitched buzz and Miss Delabole's voice came through an invisible loudspeaker. "Tea's ready, everyone!"

"All right, all right!" snapped Dr Delabole. He did not appear to be in a very good temper; still less so when he turned to see his telescope swinging wildly round on its axis with Washington hanging on to the other end of it.

"Wahee!" yelled Washington. "This is great!"

Realising at once that the RMF had come into operation Dame Barbara reached out an arm and plucked him off in mid-flight. "So sorry," she murmured. Dr Delabole muttered something under his breath they couldn't quite catch.

They found Miss Delabole waiting for them beside

a trolley laden with delicious-looking sandwiches and scones and jellies and cakes. Washington worked his way steadily through everything, but from beginning to end his eyes were fixed on an enormous white fluffy meringue with a cherry on top.

"Go on, Washington," said Miss Delabole indulgently when the trolley was almost empty. "There's no point in leaving anything."

Without hesitation Washington grabbed the meringue and stuffed it greedily into his mouth. As soon as he bit into it powdery white crumbs flew everywhere and blobs of thick cream oozed down his chin. Dr Delabole, who was sitting next to him on the black leather sofa, edged away and began dusting bits of meringue from his kaftan.

When at last Dame Barbara announced it was time to go Dr Delabole sprang to his feet, looking relieved. On their way out through the hall Washington asked if he could have one more go in the lift but Dame Barbara kept a firm grip on his shoulder and said she didn't think it would be wise after eating all those cream cakes. They thanked Miss Delabole for having them and said how much they had enjoyed their visit. Miss Delabole smiled and said it had been a pleasure. Dr Delabole said nothing.

When the door had closed behind them and the sound of the Boomsprocket died away, he turned to his sister with a thunderous expression. "You've slipped up this time, Hermione! That creature is, without a shadow of doubt, a BOY!"

Miss Delabole looked puzzled. "It does seem to *behave* like a boy – "

"He swung on my telescope and covered the sofa with meringue," grumbled her brother. "You wouldn't catch any of mine doing things like that. They obey orders, don't answer back – and above all they don't EAT!"

"Yes," she admitted, "but there's *some*thing about him . . . Anyway, I shall have an excellent opportunity to observe him in my classroom. And if there *is* a control panel in his chest I shall be able to see it when he takes his shirt off for P.E."

But Dr Delabole was not listening. He pressed a button at the side of the door and one of the mirrors slid back. A square metallic figure emerged and walked jerkily towards them, the bowl-shaped radar scanner on its head revolving slowly and giving out an eerie high-pitched whine.

"Fetch a dustpan and brush, Number Three," commanded Dr Delabole, "and clear up the crumbs you will find in the living-room."

Obediently Number Three turned and staggered off.

"Now that," declared Dr Delabole with satisfaction, "is what I *call* a robot!"

"Thank goodness that's over!" Susan heaved a sigh of relief as the steel portcullis dropped behind them and they were safely out in The Drive. "I don't like Miss Delabole much, but her brother's even worse."

"Hmmm," said Dame Barbara thoughtfully. "I wish I could have seen his laboratory. But what really intrigues me is why, when I looked through his telescope, I had such an excellent view of Arnold stooping over the marrow bed."

Chapter Ten

Washington Goes to School

"Is Washington still in the broom cupboard?" Susan asked next morning, when there was no sign of him at breakfast.

Dame Barbara nodded. "I'm leaving him there as long as possible so that his batteries are well and truly recharged. Arnold, I think you'll have to share the night watch with him this week, since he's going to spend most of the day at school."

Grandad Rammage, standing by the Whooshomatic with a plate held out waiting for bacon and eggs, muttered it would not matter anyway as nothing had happened for the last two nights and he thought the snoopers had probably given up.

"I shouldn't be too sure of that," said Dame Barbara. "After all, there's plenty of time left before the Show. They may be trying to lull you into a sense of false security."

"Pah!" Grandad Ramage gave the Whooshomatic a kick. "What's the matter with this thing? Is it going to take all day?"

"You probably put the eggs in and forgot to tell it how you want them done," said Susan. She rose from her chair and pushed the button marked FRIED. Whoosh! two slices of crispy bacon and a couple of fried eggs shot out so fast they took Grandad Ramage by surprise and he almost missed them.

Dame Barbara glanced at her watch. "You'd better give Washington a call, Susan. Do you know, I feel quite nervous at the thought of his first day at school? I hope I've fed all the right information into his

brain."

Susan felt quite nervous, too. She couldn't help wishing that Dame Barbara had left the RMF out of Washington's formula altogether.

Her fears were realised even before they reached the school building. They had just turned the corner from Mulberry Drive into the High Street when Washington pulled her sleeve and said, "You know that boy who kicked me yesterday? He's just behind us . . ."

"Don't look round," said Susan firmly. "And walk as fast as you can."

But as they reached the entrance to the playground Andy Weatherspoon caught them up. "Here, you!" He poked a finger into Washington's back. "I've got a bone to pick with you."

"Have you?" inquired Washington. "What kind of a bone?"

Susan pushed him behind her. Andy Weatherspoon was a large boy with jug-handle ears and a reputation as a bully. "Leave Washington alone!" she warned him fiercely.

"Washington! What a stupid name!" Shoving Susan aside Andy grabbed hold of Washington's arm. "Do you know what you did to my foot when you stamped on it? Turned it black and blue, you did. I reckon you owe me something for that."

By now other children had arrived in the playground and were crowding round to watch. Washington turned to smile at them in a friendly fashion and did not see Andy's fist until it landed against his jaw. For a moment he looked surprised. Then he turned to Susan and asked, "What shall I use? Karate? Judo?"

"Nothing," said Susan, trying to drag him away.

"Karate! Judo!" jeered Andy. Coming from behind he crooked his elbow around Washington's neck. "I'd like to see you try!"

The next instant Andy Weatherspoon's feet were jerked off the ground and he found himself sailing through the air. He landed at Washington's feet with a bump and sat up, looking rather surprised. The spectators cheered.

Miss Delabole appeared in the doorway and said, "You can come in now, children. I'm just going to ring the bell."

Andy struggled to his feet, complaining loudly. "He threw me over his shoulder, the rotten bully! I'm going to tell my Dad . . ."

"Good gracious, Andy," said Miss Delabole, raising her curved black eyebrows. "We all have to take a few knocks some time, you know." She patted Washington on the head as he passed her. "That's right, dear. Susan will show you where to go."

"I want to sit next to Washington," declared Nicky Potts.

"So do I," said Roy Sproggett, pleased to find someone with as big a gap between his two front teeth as himself.

"Goodness, what a popular boy he's going to be!" Miss Delabole's eyes gleamed as she followed the children into class.

She looked a little less pleased, however, when Washington brought his maths book up for correction after only three minutes. "Finished the exercise already?" she asked incredulously.

"I've finished the book," said Washington.

Miss Delabole stared down at the pages filled with neat, accurate figures. "That's very good, Washington," she murmured. "Perhaps you'd like to read while you're waiting for the others. You can choose a book from the shelves over there."

Washington chose one on astronomy and took it back to his desk. A minute later he got up from his seat again.

"Sit down!" hissed Susan from the desk behind him. "And read the book."

"I've read it," said Washington.

"Then read it again – and keep on reading till the end of the lesson."

By the time the bell went Washington had read the book twenty-seven times. He put it back on the shelf with a sigh of relief.

"I'm going to take you for Physical Education to-day," Miss Delabole announced, "so that Mr Proud-foot can have a free lesson. Hurry up and get changed."

She was already waiting for them when they came running into the gym. She stared hard at Washing-ton's bare bony chest and a frown creased her white forehead. For half-an-hour she watched him climb up ropes, hang from the wall-bars and hurtle over the vaulting-horse with centimetres to spare. By the end of the period she was looking more puzzled than ever.

During the morning break Washington was sur-rounded by a crowd of boys wanting to hear about his remarkable victory over Andy Weatherspoon. Su-san hovered anxiously nearby, trying to overhear the conversation, but Roy Sproggett noticed her and told her to go away. "We're talkin' about fightin'," he said, "and girls know nothin' about fightin' so we don't want any of 'em hangin' around, listenin' – see?"

Susan pretended to wander off towards a group of girls playing a skipping game, but as soon as she saw that the boys had forgotten about her she crept back until she was close enough to catch what they were saying.

"I wish I could do karate," sighed Nicky Potts. "I wouldn't half give my Dad a shock."

"Me too," agreed Roy Sproggett. "Could you teach us, Washington?"

"Course I could," said Washington.

"Oh, great! Let's start now . . ."

"Better not," warned Nicky Potts " 'cause I think we're bein' watched . . ." Furtively they all glanced round in time to see Andy Weatherspoon's head dodge back behind the chestnut tree in the middle of the playground. "Let's go up to the sports ground after school. Then Washington can teach us karate in secret."

"Oh no, he can't do that," said Susan, forgetting she was not supposed to be there. "Aunt Barbara said

I was to take him straight home."

They swung round to glare at her furiously. "Thought I'd told you to go away," said Roy Sproggett. "That's the trouble with this playground – spies everywhere. Come on, let's have a game of football . . ."

"What's football?" asked Washington.

Susan groaned inwardly. How *could* Aunt Barbara have failed to make sure he knew about football!

They stared at Washington as if unable to believe their ears. "Surely you know what *football* is?" said Nicky Potts at last.

Washington shook his head. "Never heard of it."

Roy Sproggett gave a low whistle. "Where've you been livin', then? The South Pole?"

In desperation Susan elbowed her way through to the centre of the group, not caring if they resented her butting in on their conversation. "He – he comes from South America," she announced, remembering Dr Stanley Blanchflower's postcard from Lake Titicaca. "I expect they don't know about football there."

"You must be joking!" exclaimed Nicky Potts. "Some of the best footballers in the world are South American."

Fortunately at this moment Miss Delabole appeared in the doorway and rang the bell for the end of break. "Silence, please, and straight back into class," she called, giving Washington an encouraging smile as he filed past her. "History next, Washington. We'll find out how much you know already, shall we?"

Washington nodded happily and when the lesson began gave the class a full account of the Battle of Hastings, right down to the last arrow. In Biology he described in detail the digestive system of the bullfrog, but when asked to write a composition entitled "My Wildest Dream" he handed in a completely empty page.

"Never mind, Washington," said Miss Delabole, by now pale with exhaustion. "It doesn't matter in the least if you can't think up a good story. Your general knowledge is excellent – almost as good as an encyclopaedia."

"How did he get on?" asked Dame Barbara as soon as they arrived home.

"Not too bad," said Susan. "Only I think you ought to take out some of the facts and put in some ideas instead. He knows an awful lot but he can't write a story. Oh, and he's never heard of football."

Dame Barbara groaned and struck her forehead with a clenched fist. "What a ninny I am! I forgot about football."

"It nearly gave us an awkward moment," said Susan, "but luckily we were saved by the bell. Also his maths is much too good. We're only on Book Two."

"Right," said Dame Barbara. "I'll make some adjustments. After all, it's only by experimenting one can attain perfection." She turned to her brother. "Isn't that so, Arnold? It's taken you years to produce the perfect marrow."

Grandad Ramage nodded. "And when you do manage something good there's always someone wanting to come along and spoil it all."

"Dear me, what a gloomy fellow you are," sighed Dame Barbara. "Why not look on the bright side for a change? You've managed to grow a good marrow and I've succeeded in inventing Washington – and nobody's going to spoil anything for either of us, if *I* have any say in the matter!"

Chapter Eleven

The Marrow Raid

Septimus Sharpe lifted his right foot from Gordon's shoulder and rubbed it against his aching calf muscle. His elbows were resting on top of the wall and his eyes glued to the moonlit figure of Grandad Ramage, who was seated on an upturned wheelbarrow with a pitchfork gripped in one hand.

"Is he still there?" inquired Gordon from below.

"Ssssh!" hissed Septimus, replacing his foot and accidentally knocking Gordon's bowler hat down over his eyes. "And keep still."

"Everything's gone dark," Gordon complained. "What's the time?"

Septimus glanced at the luminous dial of his watch. "Just on midnight."

"Past my bed-time." Gordon yawned. "How much longer, Sep?"

Septimus made no reply. He was watching Grandad Ramage's head begin to nod slowly forward until it rested on the arm that held the pitchfork. A few seconds later the silence of the night was broken by gentle snores.

"Right!" said Septimus. He raised himself up and swung one leg over the wall so that he was seated astride. "Come on, Gordon. Give us your hand."

After a good deal of pulling and heaving and scrambling and swearing Gordon joined him on top of the wall. "Where's the tape?" asked Septimus.

Gordon adjusted his hat and produced a measuring tape from his pocket.

"Hand it over, then. I'll take the measurements

while you keep an eye on the old fellow. If he stirs put somethin' over his head."

Gordon looked uncertain. "What sort of somethin', Sep?"

"Old sack, your coat – anythin' you like," said Septimus impatiently. "Just as long as you make sure he can't see who we are and what we're up to."

He slid off the wall and landed softly in a pile of dead leaves. Taking a small torch from his pocket he picked his way carefully between the cabbages, moving the thin beam of light over the ground until he found what he was looking for.

The marrow bed was a mound of earth in one corner of the garden. After a quick glance over his shoulder to make sure Gordon had landed safely, Septimus went down on his knees and lifted the leaves, shining the torch on to a magnificent striped green marrow.

"Hey, that's a big 'un," he muttered under his breath, unravelling the tape to measure its length and girth. Fumbling in his top pocket for a notebook and stubby pencil he wrote down the details and then moved forward to make a further exploration. Almost at once he discovered an even larger marrow – and another – and another, feverishly recording the vital statistics in his notebook.

Meanwhile Gordon, having landed rather less softly than Septimus in a blackberry bush, was creeping towards the motionless figure of Grandad Ramage. So intent was he on watching for any warning signs of movement that he failed to notice the rake propped up against the garden shed until his foot pressed down the metal teeth and the handle flew up and hit him with considerable force. "Sufferin' cats! Who did that?" he demanded loudly, momentarily stunned by the impact.

"Eh? What?" Grandad Ramage sat up with a jerk. His eyes went straight to the beam of light hovering over the marrow bed and the shadowy figure crouched behind it. "Here, what's going on?"

"Somethin' to cover his head," muttered Gordon,

frantically searching around for an old sack. He found instead a bucket containing potato peelings and egg shells collected from the Whooshomatic for the compost, and swiftly upended it over Grandad Ramage's shoulders.

Finding himself suddenly buried under an avalanche of rubbish Grandad Ramage let out a bellow of rage which, amplified by the bucket, sounded almost inhuman, like a wounded elephant.

Susan awoke with a start with a strange cry echoing in her ears. Surely it had come from outside . . . ?

She switched on her bedside lamp and ran to the window. In the middle of the garden, illumined by the square of light from her room, she saw Grandad Ramage jumping up and down with rage, a curly piece of potato peel hanging from one ear and a small eggshell perched on top of his head.

At the same time a window was flung open on the floor above and Dame Barbara's voice boomed out, "Stand firm, Arnold! Help is on the way."

Hastily grabbing her dressing gown, Susan flung open her bedroom door in time to see Washington hurtle down the stairs, his amber eyes flashing like Belisha beacons. She followed him at once, arriving at the back door just as he shot into the garden at top speed, pushing Grandad Ramage aside in his haste to reach the intruders.

As Susan ran up to her grandfather she noticed that his face had turned dark purple and his moustache was twitching in the most alarming fashion. "Are you all right, Grandad?" she asked anxiously.

For a moment he seemed unable to speak, then at last the words came out in a confused splutter. "They were m-measuring m-my m-m-marrows!"

"How peculiar." Susan peered into the shadows at the end of the garden, where some kind of a struggle seemed to be going on. She could just make out the figure of a tall, thin man sitting astride the wall and trying to pull a short, stout man free from Washington's ferocious grip round his legs. "Oh, hang on,

Washington!" she cried, rushing to his aid.

For a few seconds there was a violent tug-of-war. Then came a rending sound as the tall man pulled his accomplice clear and they both disappeared from sight over the wall.

"What's going on?" panted Dame Barbara, coming up at a brisk trot and waving a torch. "Have you caught them?"

"No, they've escaped," Susan told her, pink in the face with disappointment.

"But we've got these!" Washington announced triumphantly, holding up a pair of grey pin-striped trousers. "The little fat one left them behind."

"Splendid!" Dame Barbara seized the trousers and showed them to her brother, who was inspecting his marrows to make sure they had come to no harm. "Look, Arnold – find the man that fits these trousers and you've caught your criminal!"

Grandad Ramage straightened up and inspected the trousers. "They look a bit posh to me," he said. "I can't imagine who'd walk around Castle Brading dressed up in these."

"Look in the pockets, Grandad," Susan suggested. "You might find some kind of a clue."

He fished inside the right-hand pocket and drew out an envelope. He held it close to his nose. "Can't see a darned thing without me reading glasses . . ."

"Oh, give it to me," said Dame Barbara impatiently, shining her torch on to the envelope. "It's addressed to a Mr Gordon Twist, Staff Quarters, Castle Brading – there you are, I *told* you Lord Brading was mixed up in this somewhere!"

Grandad Ramage took the envelope from her and shook his head. "I still can't believe it of His Lordship, nor Nat Rumbold, come to that . . ."

"Nonetheless, Arnold, these trousers are incriminating evidence. If I were you I'd take them straight to the police."

"No," he said slowly, scratching his head. "I don't think I'll do that, not straight away. I'd like to make a few investigations of my own, first."

"Well, at least we now have proof of the marrow-raiders' identity," said Susan. "Aren't you glad we've got Washington, Grandad? We'd never have managed it without him."

Washington threw out his chest with pride. "I reckon I must be the greatest marrow-raider-catcher in the world!"

"That's enough, Washington," said Dame Barbara firmly. "I can't think why you have this tendency to boast. I'm sure it was never included in my original formula."

Susan giggled. "You said he couldn't lie, though, and it's probably true – he *is* the greatest marrow-raider-catcher in the world,"

Washington nodded agreement, his eyes gleaming.

Chapter Twelve

A Game of Football

It was Tuesday and Washington's second day at school. After some overnight adjustments by Dame Barbara he had managed to write a story about two burglars, which Miss Delabole read with interest, but Susan knew that the real test would come during the afternoon, when it was time for games.

At lunch Nicky Potts raised the subject of football again. "I can't believe you've never even *heard* of it," he told Washington. "I mean, there can't be anyone else in the entire world who's never heard of *football*!"

"He was only joking," Susan said quickly before Washington could answer. "Just pulling your leg, that's all."

Nicky Potts leant his elbow across the table in front of her so that she was excluded from the conversation. "Come on, Washington, tell us the truth. *Can* you play?"

"Of course," said Washington calmly. "I can play very well."

"What position – mid-field, striker, goalie . . . ?"

"Everywhere," said Washington.

Roy Sproggett gave a scornful laugh. "Your middle name wouldn't be Bighead, by any chance?"

Fortunately the Headmaster chose this moment to stop by their table. "Ah, now this must be the young man Miss Delabole's been telling me about," he said jovially, clapping a hand on Washington's shoulder. "Very good at maths, I hear."

Miss Delabole appeared at his side as if by magic. "His name's Washington," she said, smiling gracious-

ly, "and he's staying with Susan Ramage's family in Poplar Grove."

"Aha!" said the Headmaster, turning to look at Susan. "Cousin of yours, eh?"

"Yes, Sir, sort of," said Susan.

"Good! Splendid! Excellent!" He turned away to murmur something to Miss Delabole and Susan strained her ears to hear what he was saying. "Bit peculiar, isn't it, turning up out of the blue like that?"

"I believe he comes from South America," Miss Delabole explained smoothly. "Dame Barbara has – er – connections in South America."

"Humph!" grunted the Headmaster. "I still think it's a bit peculiar. But then the whole family's odd, if you ask me."

"Oh, I don't think so, Headmaster. Eccentric, perhaps, but not exactly . . ."

Susan couldn't catch the rest. Once again she was puzzled why Miss Delabole should try to help them by pretending Washington was quite normal when she must surely have realised by now there was something unusual about him. It was all very mysterious.

After lunch the whole class went up to the sports ground. Mr Proudfoot took the boys off to the soccer pitch while Miss Delabole kept the girls at the other end of the field for netball practice, but Susan felt she ought to keep an eye on Washington and so followed the boys at a discreet distance.

Mr Proudfoot told Nicky Potts and Roy Sproggett to pick teams and Nicky chose Washington straight away. "You can be goalkeeper," he said, "but watch Andy Weatherspoon like a hawk. He's their striker."

"Don't worry," said Washington confidently. "He won't score while I'm in goal."

"Oh, yes?" jeered Andy Weatherspoon, overhearing. "We'll see about that, shall we?"

As the game began Susan crouched on the grass behind the goal, trying to keep out of sight and hoping desperately that Dame Barbara had managed to feed all the right information into Washington's computer.

She needn't have worried. Despite Andy Weatherspoon's efforts Washington allowed not a single goal into the net, diving and swooping like a bird to make the most spectacular saves. Heartened by the remarkable performance of their goalkeeper, the rest of Nicky Potts' team played better than ever before, with the result that most of the rest of the game took place at the other end of the pitch, leaving Washington with nothing to do.

After a while he grew bored with this and when the ball eventually came his way, dribbled towards him by a member of his own team, he took the goal kick with such force and deadly accuracy that it shot straight down the entire length of the pitch and into the opposing team's net.

"Oh, well done!" shrieked Susan, leaping to her feet. "Well *done*, Washington!"

Mr Proudfoot stood in the middle of the field, staring at Washington open mouthed. Andy Weatherspoon came panting up to him, looking furious. "Sir, that's not allowed!"

"No, Sir, it's not!" protested Roy Sproggett. "And can you please tell Susan Ramage to go away? She's putting us off, hanging around like that."

Mr Proudfoot recovered swiftly and blew his whistle. "Quite right," he agreed. "Susan, go back to your netball. Miss Delabole will be wondering where you are."

Susan grinned happily and returned to the less exciting game being played by the girls at the far end of the field.

When the games period was over and they were all making their way back along the narrow pathway between the churchyard and the playground, Susan caught Washington up and inquired, "Who won?"

"We did, 6–nil," said Washington, looking pleased with himself. "And I've been chosen for the team."

Mr Proudfoot heard him and turned round to tell Susan, "That means he'll have to stay for football practice after school on Thursday."

"Congratulations, Washington," smiled Miss Delabole, who was walking beside Mr Proudfoot. "Will he be the new goalkeeper?"

Mr Proudfoot smiled. "No, I think he'd be wasted in goal. We'll probably make him striker. I've never seen such a powerful kick."

Andy Weatherspoon, following close behind, heard this remark and scowled deeply. Up till now he had always been the team's star striker and he didn't like the idea of losing his place to a new boy, particularly one who had already made him look foolish. He hung back, reluctant to listen to the other boys singing Washington's praises.

Suddenly he heard a noise. "Psst!" Looking round, he saw two men leaning over the churchyard wall, one tall and thin with red hair and the other short and plump, dressed rather oddly in blue jeans beneath a sober black jacket.

"Psst!" hissed the tall man again. "We'd like a word with you, sonny. It may be you can help us . . ."

Andy's scowl grew deeper. "I gotta get back to class."

"This won't take long. My friend here's lost some very valuable property, you see, and he's offering a substantial reward to get it back."

"A reward?" Interested now, Andy edged a little closer. "What's he lost, then?"

"His trousers."

Andy sniggered, but found himself immediately hauled up by his football shirt and held uncomfortably close to the tall man's foxy face. "We're not jokin', sonny. He needs those trousers back and he needs 'em fast."

"Okay, okay!" choked Andy, gasping for breath. "But I don't see what you expect *me* to do about it."

The short, plump man became agitated. "It was that boy who took 'em, that boy you were playin' football with just now. The one with the freckles and the yellow eyes . . ."

Andy stared at him. "You mean Washington?"

"That's the name! I heard the girl say it last night, just as he grabbed hold of me trousers."

"Steady, Gordon." The tall man fixed Andy with

a pair of steely blue eyes. "This kid . . . Washington – he a friend of yours?"

"Not exactly," said Andy cautiously.

"But you do *know* him?"

"Oh, I know him!" Andy's tone was bitter. "He just cheated me out of my rightful place in the school team. Oh yes, I know him all right!"

His captor grinned and relaxed his hold. "How'd you like to get your own back on him, then – and earn a little pocket-money into the bargain?" He drew out a wallet from inside his jacket and tapped it with a long bony finger.

Andy's eyes glinted with greed and he held out his hand.

"Oh, no! You don't get paid till afterwards." The wallet disappeared again. "Well, what do you say? Will you help us get those trousers back?"

Andy nodded, moistening his lips.

"Right, now here's what we want you to do . . ."

Chapter Thirteen
The Great Race

After school Susan took Washington home and ran upstairs to tell Dame Barbara how successful her adjustments had proved, but she was surprised to see a notice outside the laboratory saying 'DO NOT DISTURB: EXPERIMENT IN PROGRESS'.

Goodness, she thought, Aunt Barbara must have started on a new invention already.

She returned slowly to the kitchen, where Washington had already helped himself to two sausages and a large portion of chips from the Whooshomatic. "Where's Grandad?" she asked him.

"In the garden," mumbled Washington with his mouth full.

Susan sighed and picked up the pair of pin-striped trousers draped carelessly over the back of a chair. "I do wish he'd make up his mind what to do with these," she said, folding them neatly and putting them inside a carrier bag.

"He says he's still thinking about it," said Washington. "He may take them up to Mr Rumbold at the Castle and then again he may take them straight to the police station. He hasn't decided yet."

Susan extracted a cup of tea and a piece of cake from the Whooshomatic and sat down at the table. "I must get down to some housework this evening. If only Aunt Barbara would invent something that could do the ironing – " She stopped abruptly and stared at Washington. "But then I suppose she already has . . . Washington, *you* can do the ironing. There's a whole pile of shirts and jumpers and things in the

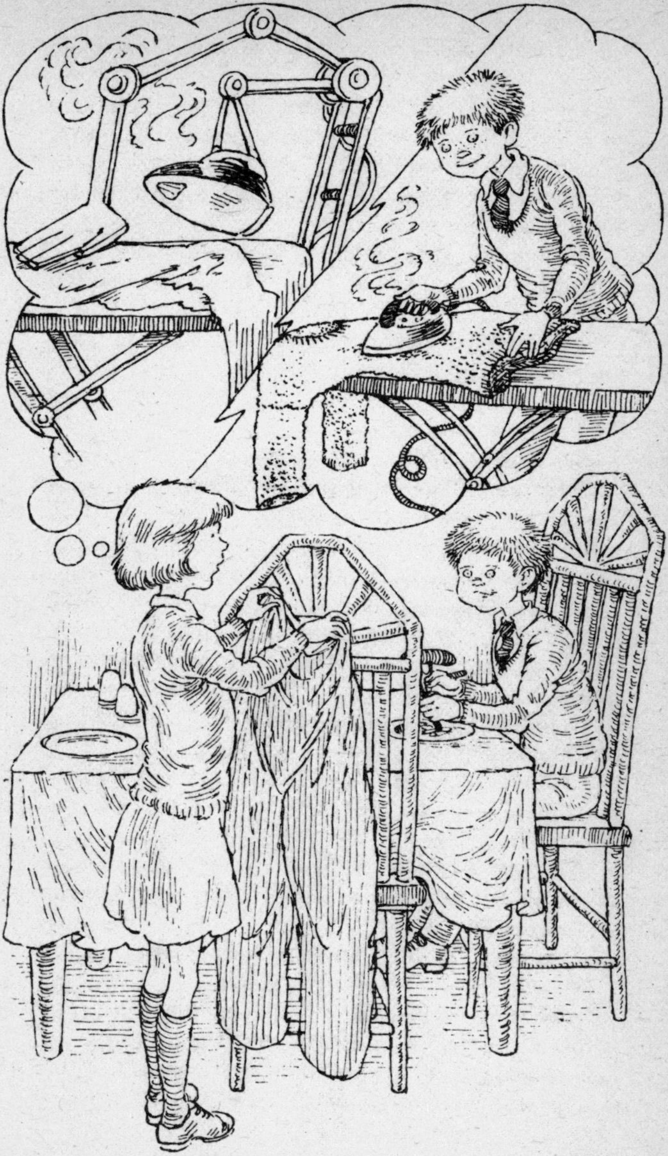

cupboard under the stairs."

"No fear," said Washington, scraping his plate clean. "That's girls' work."

"But – but Aunt Barbara said you'd be able to help me around the house," said Susan, puzzled. "After all, what's the good of a ro – " She stopped herself just in time. "I mean, you're supposed to do as you're told, Washington."

"And Nicky Potts told me I shouldn't do girls' work. He says you're too bossy. He says I'm stupid always doing what *you* tell me to do."

Susan decided she must ask Aunt Barbara to make sure that Washington only obeyed *their* instructions and not everyone else's; otherwise there was bound to be some confusion.

"Then why don't you go outside and polish the Boomsprocket?" she suggested impatiently. "At least you can't say *that's* girls' work."

He shrugged and wandered out to the garage, armed with a tin of turtle wax and a couple of cloths.

When Andy Weatherspoon stopped his bicycle outside No. 7, Poplar Grove and saw Washington in the garage, hard at work on the Boomsprocket, he congratulated himself on his good luck. He leant over the gate and called out, "Hello, Washington."

Washington swung round and his amber eyes narrowed suspiciously. "What do you want?" he demanded.

"Not very friendly, are you?" Andy gave him an oily grin. "I just happened to be passing, so I thought I'd drop in for a chat."

Washington ignored him and turned back to his polishing.

Andy propped his bicycle against the fence and opened the gate. " 'smatter of fact, I gotta favour to ask," he said, leaning one hand carelessly against the shining surface of the Boomsprocket.

"Take your mucky fingers off there," growled Washington. "I just polished that bit."

Andy's smile slipped for a moment, but he soon

recovered and followed Washington round to the back of the garage. "Fact is," he explained, "friend of mine paid a call on you last night and left his trousers behind accidental-like, so to speak."

Washington stared at him. "You mean one of the marrow raiders? Well, he can't have them back. Mr Ramage is keeping them as evidence."

Andy lowered his voice to a confidential whisper. "I don't suppose you'd happen to know where they are, right this minute?"

"Course I know," said Washington. "They're in the kitchen. Susan put them in a carrier bag."

Andy's eyes gleamed with satisfaction. "Could you get hold of 'em for me, d'you think, without anyone knowing?"

"I *could*," said Washington. "But I won't. Why should I?"

Andy hesitated. Being a very selfish boy by nature he was reluctant to offer payment of any kind, especially since he would not be receiving any money from Septimus until after his mission was completed. "Tell you what," he said, "We'll have a race, and if I win you gotta give me the trousers."

"What if *I* win?" asked Washington.

"You keep 'em, of course." Andy began to feel more confident. "Well? Is it a deal?"

Washington looked doubtful. "What sort of a race . . . a running race?"

"No, not a running race," said Andy hastily, remembering the turn of speed displayed by Washington on the soccer pitch. "A bicycle race."

"I haven't got a bicycle."

Andy was silent for a moment. Then inspiration struck him. "I know," he said, grinning broadly. "I'll ride my bike and you can drive this thing . . ." He kicked the Boomsprocket's rear bumper, secure in the knowledge that even at top speed it had never been known to exceed fifteen kilometres an hour. "That's a fair enough bargain, isn't it?"

Washington hesitated. "I don't have a licence . . . and, anyway, Dame Barbara wouldn't let me."

"She needn't know anything about it," said Andy persuasively. "Come on . . . I dare you!"

Washington looked at Andy and he looked at the Boomsprocket. Inside his head the RMF went click and he began to smile. "All right," he said at last. "All right, I will!"

Andy Weatherspoon gave a triumphant laugh. "And you promise to give me the trousers?"

"Only if you win," said Washington, checking the fuel tank to make sure it was well topped up with fresh compost.

"Oh, sure!" crowed Andy. "Now, I'll tell you the course we'll take . . ."

Sergeant Fogarty of the Castle Brading Police Force was standing by a Panda car parked in the High Street, chatting to the constable inside, when he heard a roar so deafening that he instinctively glanced heavenwards to see if they were being invaded by an alien spaceship. He soon realised, however, that the noise was coming from the direction of Chestnut Avenue, and in the next instant saw the Boomsprocket approaching the crossroads at a reckless pace, neck and neck with a large boy on a bicycle. Neither of them appeared to notice the traffic lights turning red and shot straight across the intersection, causing a milk float to pull up so abruptly it shed several crates of empty bottles on to the road.

Tight-lipped, Sergeant Fogarty flung himself into the Panda car and ordered, "Follow that steamroller!"

The ground shook as the Boomsprocket thundered along the High Street, its red-and-white awning flapping wildly in the breeze. Everyone stood still and stared in amazement. Had Dame Barbara taken leave of her senses? Her invention had always seemed such a slow, lumbering vehicle, noisy but harmless. What on earth could have happened to transform it into this terrifying monster, hurtling past them at such an alarming speed? Hardly anyone noticed the cyclist, scarlet-faced with exertion, crouched over his handlebars as he desperately battled to keep up.

The Boomsprocket swung right into The Drive so sharply that the Panda car was taken by surprise and continued some way along the High Street before finally managing to pull up. "Turn as quickly as you can!" commanded Sergeant Fogarty. "I want to catch that lunatic red-handed."

Miss Delabole, on her way home from a PTA meeting, was about to enter "The Briars" under the portcullis when she heard the Boomsprocket racketing down the hill. She looked round just in time to catch a brief glimpse of the driver as it passed her. "Oh, my goodness . . . Washington!" she exclaimed, and immediately set off in pursuit.

By now the Boomsprocket was clearly in the lead. Andy Weatherspoon saw he was losing ground steadily and lowered his head, pedalling as hard as he could down The Drive towards the towpath.

Skilfully Washington stopped the Boomsprocket less than a metre away from the sign that said 'DANGER – RIVER AHEAD'. "I've won!" he yelled gleefully.

Andy Weatherspoon, however, not realising he had reached the agreed finishing post, jammed on his brakes too late and flew over his handlebars into the river with a resounding splash.

Seconds later Miss Delabole arrived. "Washington," she panted, ignoring the plaintive cries coming from the river as she climbed up into the Boomsprocket. "What on earth were you trying to do?"

"We had a race and I won," he told her. "Andy didn't know about the extra gear, you see. Dame Barbara never uses it, not round Castle Brading. She says it could be dangerous . . ."

With a screech of brakes the Panda car drew up behind them.

"Leave this to me," Miss Delabole hissed at Washington. "Don't say a word . . ."

When Sergeant Fogarty came up to the Boomsprocket he found Miss Delabole sitting in the driving seat with Washington beside her.

"I'm most dreadfully sorry, Sergeant," she said with an apologetic smile, "but you see I've never driven this vehicle before and I didn't know about the – er – extra gear. Washington was trying to explain it to me . . ."

Sergeant Fogarty muttered something under his breath about women drivers before turning to the other policeman. "Sounds as if there's someone drowning over there," he said wearily. "You'd better take care of that, constable, while I try to sort out this little matter."

Chapter Fourteen

Gordon Pursues his Trousers

"Honestly, Washington," said Susan sternly while they were having breakfast next morning. "I don't know what would have happened if Miss Delabole hadn't come to your rescue. I only hope the police won't take her to court for jumping the traffic lights."

"Oh, they won't do that," Washington assured her. "She kept smiling at Sergeant Fogarty and saying how sorry she was and they ended up quite good friends. He told her she was a naughty girl but he'd let her off with a caution this time."

"Perhaps I was wrong to dislike her so much," said Susan thoughtfully. "She really does seem to be on our side after all, especially as she had to drive the Boomsprocket back here with Sergeant Fogarty following her to make sure she did nothing wrong." She sighed. "I do wish Aunt Barbara would come downstairs so that we could tell her about it."

There was still no sign of Dame Barbara. Susan had gone up several times to listen at the laboratory door, but all was silent. She was longing to ask her aunt to remove the RMF from Washington's formula since it was causing so much trouble, but knew better than to interrupt Dame Barbara in the middle of an experiment.

"Anyway, it was all Andy Weatherspoon's fault," Washington was saying. "He suggested we have a race because he wanted to make me give him that pair of trousers."

"Did you hear that, Grandad?" Susan turned to her grandfather, who was reading a magazine while

he ate his cereal. "Someone else is interested in those trousers now. I think Aunt Barbara's right – you ought to take them to the police."

Grandad Ramage lowered the *Vegetable Growers' Weekly* to peer at her. "Oh, very well," he said reluctantly. "I'll take 'em along this morning if it'll make you any happier."

"It certainly will." Susan started to clear the table. "Come on, Washington, or we'll be late for school."

At the end of morning break, when the other children were already returning to the classroom, Washington noticed Septimus Sharpe and Gordon Twist on the other side of the playground wall. They seemed to be trying to attract Andy Weatherspoon's attention, but he pretended not to notice them and hurried back into class with his collar turned up.

Washington was just about to follow him when Septimus beckoned him over. "Here, sonny . . . you'll do. In fact, you'll do even better. Let's cut out the middle man and get straight down to business. Like to earn yourself a bit of money?" He spun a silver coin in the air but before Washington could reach out a hand it had already vanished again. "Could be yours if you do as I say."

"If it's those trousers you want," said Washington, "you're too late. Mr Ramage is taking them to the police station this morning."

A long drawn out wail from Gordon was cut short as Septimus thumped him across the shoulders. "Shut up, Gordon. That won't do no good."

"Washington, where are you?" Miss Delabole stood in the doorway, looking round the playground. "Ah, there you are! Come along, you're late back to class." Her gaze went past him to the two men and sharpened with recognition. "Why, gentlemen – please don't go! I've been wanting to have a word with you."

She patted Washington on the shoulder as he passed her on his way into the school building and came up to the wall, giving the two men such a gleaming smile they were both transfixed.

"I believe we may have something in common," began Miss Delabole smoothly. "Shall we call it a close interest in Applied Science?"

Gordon nudged his companion. "What's Applied Science, Sep?"

"Be quiet!" snarled Septimus. To Miss Delabole he said aggressively, "No idea what you're talkin' about, ma'am."

Miss Delabole nodded. "You're right to be cautious. This is far too public a place to discuss such important matters. Could you come to 'The Briars' tonight? I'd like you to meet my brother."

"Your brother?" Septimus looked bewildered.

"It's the large house in The Drive, second on the left as you go down the hill." Miss Delabole moved nearer to add confidentially, "I'm sure you'll find it a *rewarding* visit . . ."

Septimus swallowed hard. "Rewardin'?"

"My brother is a *very* generous man. Shall we say eight o'clock?" With a little wave of the hand she departed.

"Is she a nut-case, Sep?" inquired Gordon.

"Prob'ly. Still, there's no harm in goin' along, is there? Could be our luck's turnin' at last, Gordon old son."

"Maybe so," said Gordon gloomily, "but it won't help us get me trousers back, will it?"

"We'll get 'em back, don't worry. We'll get 'em back for you this very morning . . ."

Grandad Ramage was walking up Mulberry Road towards Castle Brading High Street with the carrier bag under his arm when he became aware of footsteps behind him. He turned round but there was no-one there, so on he went, listening hard. Pad, pad – there they were again! He increased his pace, began to trot and then to run. The footsteps quickened until they were close behind him. He heard heavy breathing down the back of his neck but before he could turn round again a rough hand grabbed hold of his shoulder. "Help! Help, I'm being robbed!" he shouted at the top of his voice.

The Misses Trim, at work in their front garden, looked over the hedge and saw Grandad Ramage engaged in a fierce struggle with two men who were trying to grab a parcel from under his arm. Fearlessly Miss Evangeline rushed out of the gate, brandishing her shears. "You cowards, attacking an old man in the street!" she cried indignantly. "Leave him alone this instant."

"Leave him alone!" echoed Miss Lavinia, following with a trowel.

Miss Evangeline seized hold of the taller man's coat, pulling him away to leave Grandad Ramage locked in combat with the shorter man, who was shouting, "Those are *my* trousers! Give 'em back . . . !"

"Oh no, you don't," grunted Grandad Ramage, holding on tightly to the carrier bag.

Miss Lavinia closed her eyes and hit his assailant over the head with her trowel. He let go of the carrier bag instantly. Grandad Ramage lost his balance and sat down on the pavement.

"Come on, Gordon – beat it!" The taller man took off down the road at a loping run. His companion followed, rather unsteadily.

The Misses Trim helped Grandad Ramage to his feet and said what an outrage it was being attacked in broad daylight and in Castle Brading too, which had always been such a quiet little place. As soon as Grandad Ramage had recovered his breath he thanked them gruffly for their help and hurried on his way to the police station.

Sergeant Fogarty leant across the desk. "Hello, Arnold. How are you these days? Marrows doing well?"

"Mustn't grumble," said Grandad Ramage. "How about your gladioli?"

Sergeant Fogarty tapped the side of his nose meaningly. "I have high hopes this year, Arnold, high hopes. Now, what can I do for you?"

Grandad Ramage told him the full story. Sergeant Fogarty took out the trousers and inspected them. He looked at the envelope and shook his head sadly. "It's not like young Gordon to get mixed up in something like this. Must have fallen into bad company." He put the trousers back in the carrier bag and took it over the desk. "All right, Arnold, you leave this to me. I'll get to the bottom of it, never fear."

Chapter Fifteen

One Good Turn Deserves Another

"Marrows? Who said anything about marrows?" Dr Lucius Delabole stared at the two men facing him in the mirrored hall at "The Briars", then turned to his sister with an irritated frown. "It looks as though you've made another blunder, Hermione. These men are idiots . . ."

Septimus Sharpe's face turned as red as his hair. "Now, look here, me and Gordon have been to a lot of trouble, comin' here tonight, so don't you start callin' us no names, 'cos we're not goin' to stand for it! Are we, Gordon?"

Gordon shook his head. He had taken off his bowler hat and was nervously turning the brim round and round in his hands. He had not liked coming under the portcullis and he did not care for the mirrors either. Wherever he looked he could see so many reflections of himself and Septimus he was no longer sure which were real and which were only images. It made him feel most peculiar.

"There does seem to have been a slight misunderstanding," said Miss Delabole soothingly, "but I'm certain we can soon sort it out." She guided them across the hall into the black-and-white living room, pausing on the threshold to call over her shoulder, "Come along, Lucius."

Reluctantly her brother followed but he refused to sit down, preferring to lean against the white marble mantelpiece.

"Why don't you ring for some coffee?" Miss Delabole suggested. "I'm sure Mr Sharpe and Mr Twist would like some refreshment."

Dr Delabole pressed a black button on the white wall and spoke into a wire grille beside the fireplace. "Coffee for four, in the living room immediately."

"Now," began Miss Delabole, clasping her white hands together, "Let's get our facts absolutely clear. You are interested in No. 7 Poplar Grove because you fear that Mr Ramage's marrows may be larger than Lord Brading's. Is that correct?"

Septimus nodded.

"But what I don't understand," she continued, "is *why* you're so anxious for Lord Brading to win that Cup on Saturday?"

Septimus scowled at her, but Gordon was only too ready to explain. "That's easy," he said. "His Lordship told us that if he wins the Cup this year he's goin' to give us all a rise in our wages as a sort of celebration of his victory. Ouch!" He winced as Septimus kicked him sharply on the ankle.

"Ah!" said Miss Delabole. "Now I understand. Well, that seems a perfectly reasonable explanation to me. Don't you agree, Lucius?"

Her brother sighed impatiently.

"*We* are also interested in No. 7 Poplar Grove," she explained, "but for a quite different reason. The boy Washington . . ." She hesitated as if uncertain how to put it into words.

Gordon glanced up. "He took me trousers off me!"

"Really?" Miss Delabole looked surprised.

Gordon nodded. "When we were gettin' over the wall. Incriminatin' evidence, they are."

Miss Delabole smiled at him sympathetically. "Then would I be right in thinking you don't feel very kindly towards this – er, boy?"

Septimus and Gordon stared at her doubtfully, but they were saved from having to answer by the sound of the door sliding back and a clanking of metal.

"Bring it over here, Number Two," ordered Dr Delabole.

The robot moved towards him, carrying on its outstretched arms a tray with a jug of coffee, four cups, sugar and cream. Dr Delabole pointed to a table beside his sister's chair and the robot bent to slide the tray on to it. Then it straightened up and waited, the metal scanner on its head revolving silently.

"That is all," said Dr Delabole. "You may go."

The robot made a high bleeping noise and backed through the door, which slid noiselessly across behind it.

"Cream and sugar, Mr Sharpe?" inquired Miss Delabole.

Septimus gulped, his eyes standing out like green glass marbles. "Thank you, ma'am," he croaked at last.

"And for you, Mr Twist?"

Gordon's mouth opened twice but no sound came out. In the end he nodded, thrusting his hands deep into his pockets to hide their trembling.

"As I was saying," Miss Delabole continued, "the boy Washington is of particular interest to my brother. He wishes to carry out a closer examination under laboratory conditions. Isn't that so, Lucius?"

Dr Delabole gave her a scornful look. "I suppose so, if only to prove you must be wrong."

"I am not wrong, as you will soon discover," she told him firmly. Turning back to Septimus, she said, "The question is, are you prepared to help us? It will mean bringing the boy here, to this house, without the knowledge of Dame Barbara Blanchflower. She must not have the slightest suspicion where he has been taken, and if anything should go wrong on no account are you to mention my name – or that of my brother. Is that clear?"

Septimus cleared his throat. "How much?"

"Ah!" Miss Delabole leant back in her chair. "It would seem to me that one good turn deserves another. If you bring Washington here within the next day or so I'm quite certain it will be well within my brother's powers to ensure that Lord Brading wins that Cup next Saturday."

They all looked at Dr Delabole.

"Certainly it could be arranged," he said with a

shrug.

Septimus said suspiciously, "You mean you're goin' to nobble old man Ramage's marrows instead of us?"

Miss Delabole gave a tinkling laugh. "Good heavens, no!" She leant forward and said confidentially, "It just so happens that my brother is probably the most brilliant scientist alive today. For him it will be a simple matter to improve one of Lord Brading's marrows beyond all recognition. A little hormone injection, administered by yourselves, and it will soon be ten times bigger than any marrow produced by natural means."

Gordon's coffee cup rattled so loudly in its saucer he was forced to set it down on the table. "I don't like it," he muttered, clambering to his feet. "Let's forget the whole thing, Sep. I want to go home . . ."

Septimus pulled him back on the sofa, which made a loud snorting noise. He turned to Dr Delabole. "Right, it's a deal," he growled. "When do we get the stuff?"

"When *we* get Washington," said Miss Delabole, "and not a moment before." She added thoughtfully, "Tomorrow evening would be the best time, when he stays late for football practice. That means Susan Ramage won't be with him, so you shouldn't find it too difficult . . ."

Chapter Sixteen

Kidnapped!

When school was finished on Thursday Susan waited in the playground until Washington came out of the changing room with the rest of the team, ready for the football practice.

"Oh, no!" groaned Nicky Potts when he caught sight of her. "Not Susan Ramage again. Why does she have to keep hanging around?"

"Because she wants to look after poor little Washington, that's why," jeered Andy Weatherspoon, still smarting from the telling-off his mother had given him when he returned home soaked to the skin on Tuesday evening. "She's afraid one of us might be nasty to him!"

The others laughed and Roy Sproggett asked mockingly, "She your nursemaid, Washington?"

Washington frowned. "No, she's not," he muttered. "I can take care of myself."

Susan stood her ground. Since there was still no sign of Dame Barbara she felt responsible for Washington's safety. "I'm coming to watch the football practice," she said determinedly. "There's no law against girls watching the football practice, I suppose?"

"Well, if there isn't there ought to be," said Nicky Potts, looking disgusted. "Washington, tell her to go home, for goodness' sake."

"Go home, Susan, for goodness' sake," said Washington.

It was at this point that Miss Delabole decided to intervene. "Susan! I'd like a private word with you," she called, emerging from the school building. "Boys, you'd better hurry along to the sports ground. Mr Proudfoot will be waiting for you."

The football team beat a hasty retreat, leaving Susan alone in the playground with Miss Delabole.

"Now, dear," said Miss Delabole, coming closer. "I know you mean well, but you really must let Washington go off by himself sometimes."

Susan was so annoyed she didn't trust herself to speak in case she said something rude.

"Otherwise you'll make him look foolish in front of the other boys," Miss Delabole went on smoothly. "Naturally I can understand your anxiety . . ."

"You can?" said Susan, surprised.

"Of course, but I'm sure you've no need to worry. Washington won't come to any harm."

"It's just that he's still so *new*, you see," said Susan, adding hastily, "New to this country, I mean."

"I realise that, but he'll be all right by himself, you'll see." Miss Delabole took a firm grip of Susan's arm. "Shall we walk part of the way home together?"

It seemed to Susan she had no choice in the matter since Miss Delabole's fingers were biting into her arm like pincers. They left the playground and set off along the High Street.

After the football practice Washington stayed behind to help clear up the changing room and Mr Proudfoot gave him a serious talk about not keeping the ball to himself all the time. "Sometimes you have to pass it to another member of the team," he explained.

"But no-one else is as good as I am," said Washington, rather puzzled.

"That doesn't matter," said Mr Proudfoot, who was feeling a little puzzled himself. "It's supposed to be a team game, you see. Still," he went on cheerfully, "I'm sure that when we've sorted out some of these minor problems you're going to be a very good soccer player, Washington. In fact, I'll be surprised if we don't make mincemeat of every other school within miles of Castle Brading. Run along home, now."

When Washington came out of the school buildings into the High Street he saw Septimus Sharpe and Gordon Twist leaning against the playground wall. As he drew level with them Septimus stuck his large booted foot across the pavement and Washington nearly tripped over it. "What did you do that for?" he demanded, when he had recovered his balance.

"Oh, I *am* sorry, young sir. It's these big feet of mine, you see – always gettin' in people's way, they are."

Washington shrugged and started to walk on but Septimus shot out a bony hand to grip his shoulder. "Not so fast, sonny. Me and Gordon'd like a quiet word with you."

"Not now," said Washington, pulling away from him. "I've got to go straight home."

On the opposite side of the road Sergeant Fogarty heard their raised voices and looked up from the conversation he was having with the constable on point duty.

Septimus took a coin from his pocket and held it out invitingly on the palm of his hand. "Remember that little conversation we had the other day?"

"I remember," said Washington, his eyes fixed on the shiny coin, "but the police have already got your trousers."

Gordon cast an uneasy glance across the road at Sergeant Fogarty and nudged Septimus. "That copper's watchin' us, Sep. I'm scared . . ."

"Be quiet!" snarled Septimus. With a rapid change of expression he turned his yellow grin on Washington again. "It so happens there's another little matter we'd like to discuss with you. Surely you wouldn't say no to a bit of extra pocket money?"

"Of course I wouldn't," Washington agreed. "What's the quiet word?"

"Oh, I can't tell you here," said Septimus. "It ain't quiet enough here, in the High Street. Why don't we walk along home with you down Sycamore Lane?"

"I usually go down Chestnut Avenue," said Washington. "It's quicker that way."

"That'd be no good," grumbled Gordon, who was becoming restless. "We've got to go down Sycamore Lane, 'cause that's where we left the van – OW!"

Septimus caught him a swift blow round the head and grinned at Washington. "Sycamore Lane – or no money," he growled.

Washington stared at the coin. "All right," he said, "I'll come down Sycamore Lane, if you like."

"There's a good lad," grinned Septimus. "Come on, then, let's make it snappy."

Across the road Sergeant Fogarty saw them walking off together in a friendly fashion and resumed his conversation with the police constable.

Sycamore Lane curved round behind the churchyard, running between the sports ground on one side and the high wall of the Vicarage on the other. It was overhung with dark trees and as usual deserted. When they were half-way down Washington stopped and said, "This is quiet enough. What's the word?"

"Just a little further," said Septimus, taking hold of his arm. "As far as the corner, where that blue van is parked."

"No," said Washington impatiently. "Tell me here."

"Grab him, Gordon, while I get the rope," muttered Septimus, making for the van.

Gordon did as he was told and seized Washington round the waist, pinning his arms to his sides. Washington bent down, intending to throw his attacker over his head, but Gordon was too heavy for him. His feet came off the ground but he remained precariously balanced on Washington's back. "Hurry up, Sep," he called, waving his feet in the air. "I can't hold on to him much longer . . ."

Septimus returned with a length of rope and a blanket, which he threw over both of them. Startled by the enveloping blackness Gordon released his hold and Washington fought to escape the blanket, but found his ankles immediately seized by Septimus and landed on the ground with a thud. "Tie him up!" yelled Septimus.

Gordon emerged from the blanket, retrieved his bowler hat which had rolled into the gutter, and picked up the rope.

"Get a move on," Septimus urged. "He's wrigglin' like an octopus with fleas."

Finding it difficult to get close to Washington, whose arms were flailing wildly in all directions, Gordon threw the blanket over him again and began winding the rope roughly round his chest.

"Good lad," grunted Septimus, letting go of Washington's ankles to assist him. Between them they managed to bind him up like an Egyptian mummy until he could no longer move hand or foot. Then they lifted him, ignoring the angry cries coming from under the blanket, and bundled him headlong into the back of the van.

Septimus slammed the doors shut with satisfaction and got into the driving seat.

"Here, Sep," said Gordon, breathing heavily as he sat down beside him, "did you see that kid's eyes when we were tryin' to put the blanket over his head? Like a couple of flippin' fog-lamps, they were."

Septimus switched on the ignition. "You know what your trouble is, Gordon? You're too fanciful by 'alf."

"Maybe I am, but there's somethin' about this business I don't like," said Gordon obstinately. "I don't trust that doctor – nor his barmy sister. What do they want the kid for, anyway?"

Septimus turned the van out of Sycamore Lane into Chestnut Avenue. "None of our business, is it? We hand him over, no questions asked, and in return we get the stuff to pump into his Lordship's marrow."

"And *that* ain't natural, neither," grumbled Gordon. "Who ever heard of givin' a marrow an injection to make it grow?"

"You want that rise in your wage packet, don't you? Then shut up!"

Gordon relapsed into a sulky silence as the van headed along the High Street towards The Drive.

Chapter Seventeen

Looking for Washington

Susan took a deep breath and then knocked on the laboratory door.

"Come in," said Dame Barbara's voice, slightly muffled.

Susan pressed the button and the door slid open. She stepped inside and looked round curiously. There was no sign of any new invention as far as she could see and Dame Barbara was lying on the divan bed with Moffatt across her feet and an icepack on her forehead. She did not move as Susan entered but merely murmured, "Good boy, Washington. Go straight to the broom cupboard and plug yourself in."

"It's not Washington, Aunt Barbara. It's me, Susan. I'm sorry to interrupt you in the middle of an experiment, but . . ."

Dame Barbara removed the icepack and sat up. "It's all right, Susan, I'm still at the thinking stage. Is anything wrong?"

"It's just that Washington hasn't come home yet and I'm very worried," Susan explained. "He stayed late at school for a football practice and I wanted to stay as well but Miss Delabole made me come home. She said I was making him look silly in front of the other boys by following him round all the time, but now I wish I hadn't listened to her because it's dark outside and he might have got lost . . ." Her voice trailed away miserably.

Dame Barbara swung her legs off the bed and stood up. "Don't worry," she said calmly. "He probably won't come to any harm but we'll go and look for him, just in case. Come on."

Susan heaved a sigh of relief and followed her aunt downstairs to the kitchen.

"You stay here, Arnold," Dame Barbara told her brother, "and if Washington comes back while we're gone say BROOM CUPBOARD straight away. That'll make sure he stays in one place and doesn't try to come after us."

Grandad Ramage said he would if he happened to see him but he was going to be very busy watching his marrows tonight. It was getting dangerously near the Show and he didn't trust those villains farther than the end of his nose.

They began by retracing the route Washington would have taken from school, but when they turned the corner from Chestnut Avenue into Mulberry Road they met Sergeant Fogarty on his way home. He asked them to give Grandad Ramage a message about the trousers he had handed in. "Tell him I've not done anything about them yet because I thought it best to wait until Lord Brading comes home tomorrow," he said. "It seems to me he ought to take some responsibility for the matter."

Dame Barbara agreed with him. "By the way," she added, just as he was about to walk on, "I suppose you haven't set eyes on young Washington, have you? Only he stayed late at school for a football practice and hasn't come home yet."

Sergeant Fogarty stroked his chin. "Would that by the little lad who was out with Miss Delabole in that infernal machine of yours the other evening?"

Dame Barbara looked surprised as she hadn't yet heard about Washington's escapade in the Boomsprocket, but Susan nodded quickly and said, "Yes, that's the one."

"Well, now, it so happens that I saw him having an argument with Septimus Sharpe and young Gordon in the High Street about an hour ago. I took a second look at them because of this trouser business, but just when I was wondering if I should step over the road and investigate they seemed to sort it all out and go off quite friendly-like."

Dame Barbara asked faintly, "You mean, Washington went off with the two men?"

Sergeant Fogarty nodded. "They turned down Sycamore Lane." He looked anxious. "Perhaps I should have intervened after all. Would you like me to go over to Castle Brading straight away and check up on Septimus and young Gordon?"

"Oh, no!" said Dame Barbara hastily. "No, there's no need for anything like that. In fact, I just caught a glimpse of Washington going past the end of the road on his way home, so we can't take up any more of your time, Sergeant."

He looked relieved and bade them goodbye.

"Goodness!" said Susan when he was out of earshot. "For one awful moment I thought those men might have kidnapped Washington. Thank heaven you saw him go past . . ."

"I didn't," said Dame Barbara grimly, "but we can't risk the police setting up a full-scale search. That would bring us a barrage of unwanted publicity and I'm nowhere near ready yet to launch my invention on the world. There are many more tests I have to make before that. No, Susan, we must deal with the matter ourselves."

Susan turned pale. "But where would they have taken him? Shall we go up to Castle Brading and start searching the grounds?"

Dame Barbara shook her head. "Useless, now that it's dark. He'll be well hidden, you can depend on that. No, I think we'd better go home in case they get in touch with us to make a ransom demand. I expect it's the marrows they really want."

Susan stared at her great aunt. "We can't just go home as if nothing's happened. He'll be so scared . . ."

Dame Barbara looked down at Susan's worried face and smiled. "Washington won't be scared. I told you, he isn't capable of fear. You still think of him as a real boy, don't you?"

"He *seems* like a real boy," said Susan. "And even

if he isn't scared he must be wondering where we are and why we haven't come to save him."

Dame Barbara sighed. "I know how you feel, Susan. I'm fond of the little fellow too, but you can be sure he's not missing us half so much as we're missing him. Anyway," she added briskly, "you surely don't imagine I haven't allowed for this kind of mishap? It won't be long before our kidnappers – whoever they may be – discover they've bitten off more than they can chew!"

Chapter Eighteen

Dr Delabole Examines Washington

Meanwhile Washington, relieved to find his head no longer covered by a blanket, wandered around Dr Delabole's laboratory inspecting the paraphernalia laid out on the benches. He fiddled with test tubes, shook bottles of gaseous liquid until they threatened to explode and peered curiously at the metal welding equipment. Dame Barbara certainly had nothing like that in her laboratory, but then of course Dr Delabole would need it to construct the curious creatures standing stiffly to attention against the walls, like empty suits of armour. Washington tried speaking to one of them but there was no reply.

"Must be switched off," he muttered to himself and opened a metal flap in the chest to find the controls.

"Leave that alone, boy!" roared Dr Delabole, "and come over here this instant."

In the centre of the laboratory was an operating table under an array of powerful arc lamps. Beside it Dr Delabole, in a long green surgeon's gown, was setting out a variety of surgical instruments on a trolley, assisted by Miss Delabole, who was wearing a white overall and a mask over her nose and mouth.

Obediently Washington approached the table.

"Lie down," ordered Dr Delabole.

"On the table?" asked Washington, surprised.

"Do as I say and don't argue!"

Washington lay down on the table and Dr Delabole picked up a sharp, gleaming scalpel. Then he hesitated. "It's not normal, this answering back. If you've made a mistake, Hermione . . ."

Miss Delabole smiled behind her mask. "All you have to do is find the control panel. That will prove I'm right." She leant over and pulled up Washington's sweater to uncover his chest.

Dr Delabole's scalpel wavered scarcely a centimetre away from the amazingly life-like flesh. Suddenly he peered closer and said, "I can see little blue veins. Supposing he bleeds – "

"What if he does? It's not like you to be squeamish, Lucius. Hurry up and make the incision."

"If we're charged with murder I shall lay the blame entirely at your door," said her brother. The tip of his blade pressed against Washington's skin. Again he hesitated. "Supposing the control panel isn't located in the chest after all?"

"Why don't you ask him? He always tells the truth."

Dr Delabole cleared his throat. He was not used to asking questions of robots. "Now – er – Washington. Tell me, where is your control panel?"

"Under my left foot," replied Washington.

Dr Delabole raised his black eyebrows. "How very unusual." He pulled down Washington's sweater with a sigh of relief. "In that case – "

Swiftly Miss Delabole removed the shoe and sock from Washington's left foot, which at first sight appeared perfectly normal. She began to probe delicately underneath. Washington giggled and Dr Delabole looked at him sharply.

"Sorry," said Washington, "but she tickled me."

Miss Delabole peeled back a cunningly designed flap of skin to reveal the complicated set of knobs and dials set into the sole of his foot, and beside it the socket where he plugged in to recharge his batteries. "Fascinating," she breathed. "And so ingenious . . ."

The scalpel was only a hair's breadth away from Washington's foot when Dr Delabole said suddenly, "If he's ticklish that must mean he has a built-in nervous system, in which case he's capable of feeling pain. Perhaps we should give him some kind of an anaesthetic . . ."

Miss Delabole sighed impatiently. "How many times do I have to remind you, Lucius, that he's only a robot?"

"I'm *not* a robot," said Washington indignantly. "I'm a boy!"

Dr Delabole swung round to glare at his sister. "Did you hear that? I thought you said he could only speak the truth . . ."

"Nonsense, Washington!" snapped Miss Delabole. "Of course you're a robot. You've a control panel . . ."

"Hasn't everyone?" said Washington.

Miss Delabole looked a little uncertain. "I think perhaps . . . he doesn't know," she said in a low tone to her brother.

"There's something wrong here," murmured Dr Delabole, shaking his head. "You can't tell me that Dame Barbara hasn't fitted him with some kind of a warning system, yet he's showing no sign of alarm. I think we should check whether or not there's a defence mechanism, otherwise we could be blown to kingdom come."

"Is there a defence mechanism?" Miss Delabole asked Washington.

"Of course. If you break the circuit while I'm still functioning it will cause a violent electrical reaction and you'll both be burnt to a cinder," Washington told them complacently.

Hastily Dr Delabole put the scalpel behind his back.

"So how do we switch you off?" inquired his sister.

"I respond only to two words."

"Which two words?"

Washington shook his head. "I'm programmed not to reveal them."

Petulantly Dr Delabole flung the scalpel on to the floor. "I told you it wouldn't work! Dame Barbara's no fool – we might have guessed she'd take precautions against possible capture. Now we can do nothing unless we discover those two words . . ."

"Keep calm, Lucius," said Miss Delabole in a

soothing voice. "It shouldn't be all that difficult to find out what they are. I'm sure you'll think of a way."

Chapter Nineteen

The Missing Link

When Lord Brading returned from his holiday at noon on Friday he went straight to the vegetable garden. "What news of the marrows, Nat?" he asked his head gardener. "Have we a good specimen to enter for the Show tomorrow?"

Nat Rumbold looked uncomfortable. "There is *one*, your Lordship – " he began uncertainly.

"Splendid! Let's have a look at it, then."

Silently Nat showed him the gigantic marrow that lay like a stranded whale across the vegetable garden. Lord Brading stared at it, his gooseberry-green eyes nearly popping out of his head.

"It just sort of happened overnight, milord," Nat explained. "I've never seen anything like it before, not in all my years as a gardener."

Lord Brading advanced cautiously and laid a hand on the marrow. "Feels firm and healthy, just as a marrow ought." A delighted smile spread slowly over his face. "I reckon we've done it this time, Nat! Arnold Ramage'll never manage to produce anything bigger than that!"

"No, milord," agreed Nat. "But . . ."

"Hey, you chaps!" Lord Brading had spotted two heads peering over the wall and recognised his gamekeeper and one of his footmen. "Ever seen a marrow that size before?"

Sheepishly Septimus Sharpe and Gordon muttered no, they had never set eyes on a marrow that size anywhere before.

Lord Brading gave a shout of triumphant laughter.

"Looks like you'll all be getting that rise I promised you." He saw Sergeant Fogarty and a constable coming through the gate and beckoned them over to have a look.

Sergeant Fogarty gave the marrow a surprised but fleeting glance before his gaze moved swiftly to Septimus and Gordon, who were already beginning to back away. "Sorry to trouble you, my lord," he said, "but with your permission there are a few questions I'd like to ask a couple of your staff."

"Run for it, Gordon!" hissed Septimus, and they both took to their heels, making for the river.

"After them!" yelled Sergeant Fogarty, setting off in hot pursuit, followed by the constable.

"Bless my soul!" exclaimed Lord Brading, looking puzzled. "Now what was all that about, Nat?"

Before Nat Rumbold had a chance to tell him a large figure in a royal blue tracksuit hoisted itself over the wall.

"Confounded nuisance!" muttered Dame Barbara. "I've been tracking those two chaps all morning and now that wretched policeman has frightened them off."

Lord Brading stared at her in amazement and then hastily stood in front of the giant marrow, holding out his wide check trousers in an attempt to screen it from her eyes. "Good day to you, Dame Barbara," he said. "This is an unexpected pleasure. May I inquire the purpose of your visit . . . ?"

"No time to explain," she panted, descending from the wall. "Have to push on. Any objection to my searching your grounds?"

"None at all," murmured Lord Brading, relieved she did not appear to have noticed the marrow. "Please do."

He watched her disappear into the orchard and exchanged puzzled glances with his head gardener. "Looks like there've been some rum goings-on while I've been away, Nat. Perhaps you'd better tell me about them . . ."

When Susan returned from school that afternoon she ran straight upstairs to the laboratory, where she found Dame Barbara standing on her head, deep in meditation. "Any news?" she gasped.

It took Dame Barbara several moments to come out of her trance. She lowered her feet to sit cross-legged on the floor. "Nothing definite," she said at last. "I spent the morning following our two villains until Sergeant Fogarty spoiled it all by frightening them off. Still, at least it gave me a chance to search every hut and dwelling on the estate where they might have been holding Washington prisoner."

"Did you find anything?"

"No. In fact I'd go so far as to say that he's no longer in their possession – which means they must have handed him over to someone else." Dame Barbara glanced at Susan's worried face. "I suppose you didn't discover anything at school?"

Susan shook her head. "The other children asked where he was but I said he had a cold so you were keeping him at home today."

"Good. At least people won't start getting too concerned about his disappearance."

Thoughtfully Susan stroked Moffatt's thick orange fur. "Aunt Barbara, how long can Washington go without recharging his batteries?"

"Ah, that's just the trouble." Dame Barbara sighed. "He'll be all right for twenty-four hours, but after that they'll begin to weaken and finally run down altogether. So we *must* find him tonight . . ."

Susan nodded miserably. Then her eye was caught by the blackboard on which Dame Barbara always jotted down her formulas. Today she had written some words arranged in two columns. In the first column was written MARROWS, VILLAINS, LORD BRADING, FLOWER SHOW and in the second FOOTBALL PRACTICE, WASHINGTON, VILLAINS, KIDNAP. But right in the centre between the two columns she had written the one word DELABOLE.

"That reminds me," said Susan, "Miss Delabole

didn't come into school today. The headmaster took most of our lessons."

"Aha!" Dame Barbara sprang to her feet. "Now that *is* interesting!"

"Why have you written her name on the board?" Susan asked.

"Guesswork. There has to be a connecting link between those two columns. I've no definite clue, but the more I ponder on the matter the more convinced I become that Dr Delabole and his sister are at the bottom of the whole affair. Their interest in Washington, that invitation to tea, the telescope trained on our house . . ."

"But *why*?" Susan looked puzzled. "Do you think they suspect anything?"

"It's possible. After all, Dr Delabole's a scientist and therefore perhaps the most likely person in Castle Brading to recognise Washington for what he is. I wish I could have seen inside that laboratory . . ."

They were interrupted by a knock at the door. Grandad Ramage's face appeared. "Sergeant Fogarty's downstairs, asking if you can spare him a moment."

"Botheration!" exclaimed Dame Barbara. "How that man keeps getting in my way!"

They found Sergeant Fogarty in the kitchen, gazing in wonderment at the Whooshomatic which had just furnished him with a cup of tea.

"How kind of you to call, Sergeant," said Dame Barbara graciously. "Have you had any luck in tracking down Arnold's marrow raiders?"

"I certainly have," said Sergeant Fogarty with pride. "They are at this very moment down at the Station where they've been assisting us with our inquiries. During the course of my questioning, however, some rather odd facts have come to light."

"Indeed?" said Dame Barbara encouragingly.

Sergeant Fogarty sipped his tea and cleared his throat. "Now, when I met you yesterday evening, Dame Barbara, you told me you were looking for a young gentleman called Washington, but since you did not contact me further I assumed the young gentleman in question had returned safely?"

"Quite safely, thank you," said Dame Barbara.

Sergeant Fogarty frowned. "You're certain of that?"

"Yes, of course. Why do you ask?"

"Because Septimus Sharpe and Gordon Twist told me they'd kidnapped him."

"Good gracious," said Dame Barbara. "Whyever should they say a thing like that?"

"Told me they did it in return for a favour." Sergeant Fogarty shook his head, looking mystified. "Just about the tallest story I ever heard in my life. Still, I suppose I'd better go on up to 'The Briars' and have a word with Dr Delabole."

"Dr Delabole?" queried Dame Barbara sharply.

"Oh, I daresay it'll turn out to be as much of a fairy story as the kidnapping of young Washington." Sergeant Fogarty set down his empty beaker on the table. "But one's obliged to check up on these things."

"Quite so," Dame Barbara agreed.

As soon as the door closed behind him she thumped her fist triumphantly on the table. "There you are, Susan! I told you the Delaboles were mixed up in it somewhere. They must have bribed our two villains to do the kidnapping for them."

White faced, Susan stared at her great aunt. "What are we going to do?"

"Wait until dark," said Dame Barbara, "and then pay a little visit to 'The Briars' . . ."

Chapter Twenty

Battle of the Robots

"But how on earth are we going to get in?" whispered Susan, staring up at the portcullis.

"Don't go too near," Dame Barbara warned, "or you'll trigger off the alarm." She shone her torch into the brambles and said doubtfully, "We could try cutting our way through, I suppose."

At that moment a sweep of headlights came towards them down the drive.

"What luck!" exclaimed Dame Barbara. "We should be able to dodge through when the barrier lifts for the car to drive underneath."

They pressed themselves close to the side of the entrance as the steel mesh barrier slid upwards and the car passed through, Sergeant Fogarty crouched over the wheel. The next instant they were safely inside.

"Make for the house," hissed Dame Barbara as the barrier fell with a crash behind them, "and keep to the shadows."

They had gone only a short distance when they heard a steady tramp, tramp behind them. Dame Barbara grabbed hold of Susan and together they hid behind a rhododendron bush, holding their breath.

There was a strange metallic sound about the footsteps, as if someone were walking around with a bucket on each foot. Then a large square figure moved into a pool of light coming from a window and stood still, the circular disc on its head revolving rapidly as it scanned its surroundings.

"So *that*'s it!" Dame Barbara muttered. "How

could I have been so dim-witted as not to rumble it before? Susan, give me your anorak."

Her eyes fixed in fascination at the weird figure only a few feet away Susan took off her anorak and handed it to her great aunt. "Is it a robot?" she whispered.

Dame Barbara nodded. "Of a most primitive design. But now at least we know why Dr Delabole is so interested in Washington . . ." With surprising agility she leaped out from behind the bush and flung the anorak over the robot's head. It was immediately thrown into confusion and began to turn round in circles, waving its arms wildly, but within a few seconds Dame Barbara had located the master control and switched off the mechanism. The robot stood motionless.

"Bring me the torch," said Dame Barbara.

While Susan directed the light steadily on to the robot's chest Dame Barbara took out a screw-driver from the pocket of her tracksuit and began to make adjustments to the control panel. "I do believe," she said, with quiet satisfaction, "that we may be able to put this hotch-potch of old tin cans to good use after all . . ."

Inside Dr Delabole's laboratory Washington was sitting on the operating-table, swinging his legs and yawning with boredom.

Beside him Dr Delabole was perched on a stool, reading aloud from a large dictionary. "Brontosaurus, bronze, brooch, brood . . ."

"I'm hungry," said Washington.

Dr Delabole looked helplessly at his sister. "He says he's hungry."

Miss Delabole, who was thumbing through a book called *Secret Codes and How to Break Them* said, "Perhaps it would be best to feed him. After all, we want to keep him in good working order until we've had a chance to discover the formula."

"Chicken and chips," said Washington. "That's what I want. With tomato ketchup."

Dr Delabole snapped his fingers and gave the order to a robot, which disappeared through the sliding door. Minutes later it reappeared with a plate of undercooked chicken and some soggy chips.

"What *you* need is a Whooshomatic," said Washington, gazing with disgust at the tray set before him.

Dr Delabole sighed impatiently. "Now perhaps we can get on." He ran his thumb down the page of the dictionary. "Where did I get to? Ah, yes – brood, brook, broom, broth – "

"Stop!" exclaimed Miss Delabole. "I'm certain he reacted to one of those words. Read them again."

"Brood, brook, broom . . ."

"BROOM – that's the one!" Miss Delabole declared triumphantly. "But he said there were two words. It must be broom something . . ."

"But broom what? Broom-handle? Broom-stick?" As Dr Delabole said each word he glanced at Washington, who had stopped eating and was looking watchful.

"Try cupboard," suggested his sister.

Dr Delabole tried it. Washington immediately sprang off the table, throwing the chicken and chips all over the floor.

"That's it!" cried Miss Delabole. "BROOM CUPBOARD!"

"Then why is he still working?" demanded her brother angrily. "Surely that was the signal to switch himself off?"

Spurred by the two vital words, Washington gave Dr Delabole a violent push that sent him spinning round on his stool. He ran to the sliding door and began to hammer on it. "Let me out! I've got to go home . . ." His fingers searched for the button that would open the door.

"Better not touch him, Hermione," warned Dr Delabole. "He may be dangerous."

"Don't worry, I'm taking no chances." Swiftly Miss Delabole moved to a vast switchboard and changed all the plugs from blue sockets to red sockets. "The robots are now on full alert. Let them take over."

Dr Delabole's eyes gleamed. "Why not?" he said softly. "Let us see which is the strongest – Dame Barbara's invention or mine. Robots – attack!"

There was a rumbling, creaking noise as from every side of the laboratory the robots stepped forward and began to advance on Washington.

"You can't escape!" gloated Dr Delabole, rubbing his hands gleefully. "When my sister alerted the robots she also sealed every possible exit."

Suddenly there came a crash of metal against metal and a mailed fist appeared through the door. Dr Delabole stared disbelievingly as the fist moved up and down and from side to side, until the door was in splinters, revealing the robot which stood outside. "What on earth are you doing, Number Seven?" he demanded, as it raised its arm for a final blow at the shattered metal. "You're supposed to be patrolling the garden."

Number Seven brought its fist down with relentless force and stepped through the hole it had made. It stood before Dr Delabole with its scanner revolving at twice the normal speed.

"Something's wrong!" hissed Miss Delabole. "It's been tampered with!"

"Impossible!" Dr Delabole stretched out a hand towards Number Seven's control panel but the robot struck it away.

"Lucius, take care – it's out of control!" screamed Miss Delabole.

As the robot drew back its arm to strike Dr Delabole dived for cover beneath a workbench, closely followed by his sister. "Seize Number Seven!" he shouted at the other robots. "Seize and destroy!"

During the next minutes there followed a battle of horrific volume, as Number Seven met the onslaught of its fellows in a grinding, hammering, battering clash of mindless force. Robot arm swung against robot leg, scanner met scanner head-on and gradually the air filled with smoke as one electrical circuit after another caught fire.

Choking with the fumes Dr Delabole and his sister crouched beneath the bench, covering their ears as the terrifying din went on and on. Every now and then a cog or a screw rolled in their direction, but it was impossible to tell which robot it had come from. The scene was utter confusion, a moving jungle of battered machinery bent on destroying everything in its path.

At last the noise died down to a mere jangle. A scanner rolled across the floor and spun slowly to a halt. Dr Delabole and his sister crawled out from beneath the bench to survey the destruction. The floor was strewn with crumpled, ravaged bits of metal. Not a single robot was left in one piece. Lengths of wire lay smouldering gently amidst the fragments of tubes and bottles swept from the benches during the battle. Smoke hung over the remains like a ghostly fog.

Miss Delabole stretched out a sympathetic hand to her brother. "Lucius . . ." she began.

He pushed her away roughly. "Where's Washington?" he demanded.

"Gone," said his sister. "Escaped . . ."

Dr Delabole clenched his fist and slammed it furiously against the ruined switchboard. A blue flash lit up the room, followed by a deafening explosion.

Dame Barbara and Susan, crouched in the bushes, heard the noise and exchanged anxious glances. Then something hurtled past them, racing down the drive.

"Washington!" Dame Barbara set off after him. "It's all right, Washington. We're here."

But he paid no heed to either of them. By the time Susan reached the entrance, close on Dame Barbara's heels, he had climbed half-way up the barrier. "What about the alarm system?" panted Susan.

"Should think that last explosion fused the whole works," said Dame Barbara, hoisting herself on to the wire. She called out to Washington, who by now was sitting on the top, his amber eyes shining in the dark. "Wait for us, old chap. You're quite safe now."

"Got to go straight back to the broom cupboard,"

he muttered, and leapt off the barrier.

"Great heavens, they must have hit on the safety factor!" exclaimed Dame Barbara. "I shall have to change the code . . ."

She stretched out a helping hand to Susan, but long before they were over the portcullis Washington was already running down The Drive towards Poplar Grove and the broom cupboard as fast as he could go.

Chapter Twenty-One
The Flower Show

On Saturday morning Susan accompanied her grandfather to the marquee on Castle Brading village green and helped him set out his largest marrow so that it showed to best advantage. She glanced critically at the other marrows on show and whispered, "Yours is definitely bigger than anyone else's. Which is Lord Brading's?"

"I don't think it's arrived yet." Grandad Ramage patted his own marrow proudly. "But I reckon he'll have a hard job to beat that one."

Suddenly the subdued murmur of voices inside the tent rose to an excited babble as Nat Rumbold entered backwards, carrying one end of a gigantic marrow. Supporting the other end was the second gardener from the Castle. Both men were red-faced with exertion and staggering under the weight. Between them they managed to heave the marrow on to the trestle table, which promptly collapsed.

It took the steward some time to set up the display again, and eventually he had to add another table on the end since Lord Brading's marrow took up so much room. Susan stared at it incredulously.

"Well, Arnold?" inquired Nat Rumbold, still puffing. "What do you think of *that*?"

Grandad Ramage shook his head and said slowly, "Never seen anything like it in my life. What's the secret, Nat?"

Nat shrugged. "Blowed if I know. One of Nature's flukes, I suppose."

Sergeant Fogarty came up behind them. "Remarkable sight, isn't it, Arnold? Almost makes me believe that cock-and-bull story Septimus Sharpe told me.

Susan was longing to ask what cock-and-bull story but Dame Barbara had warned her to be cautious. So far there had been no opportunity to find out from Washington exactly what had happened to him on the previous evening because he had been in the broom cupboard ever since, recharging his badly run-down batteries.

"Incidentally," Sergeant Fogarty went on, "I've released both men for the time being as I've no really good reason for holding them, unless you want to charge them with breaking and entering your premises?"

"Not much point now," said Grandad Ramage gloomily.

"Right, then. Hello, what was that?" Sergeant Fogarty glanced round at the table laden with vegetables. "Thought I heard a sort of groaning noise . . ."

"Perhaps the table's collapsing again," suggested Susan, and they all went down on their hands and knees to peer underneath, but the trestles looked firm enough.

Sergeant Fogarty stood up and dusted the knees of his trousers. "There's still a few moments before the judging," he said, "so I think I'd better just check my gladioli aren't beginning to droop."

As he turned away Dame Barbara entered the marquee, accompanied by Washington.

"Hello, Arnold," she said, coming straight over to them. "You're not looking too happy. Is Lord Brading's marrow bigger than yours after all?"

Wordlessly Grandad Ramage pointed to the monstrous specimen taking up most of the room. Dame Barbara put on her spectacles to peer at it. "Great heavens above! I reckon that ought to go into the *Guinness Book of Records*!"

"Just thinking that myself, dear lady."

They turned round to see Lord Brading, his face even redder than usual and wearing a broad smile.

Hovering close behind him was the lean, wiry figure of Septimus Sharpe and the plumply smiling Gordon, once more respectably clad in his pin-striped trousers and bowler hat.

"Looks like we've walloped you this year, Ramage, but no hard feelings, eh?"

Grandad Ramage shook Lord Brading's outstretched hand and tried to smile bravely, but it was a weak effort.

"Hope you remembered to bring the Cup along," said Lord Brading, glancing at the table. "Ah, there it is. Cleared a space for that on my mantelshelf this morning." He beamed happily round at the little crowd of people gathering to stare at the amazing sight.

Susan nudged Dame Barbara. "Look who's just arrived," she whispered.

Dr Delabole pushed his way through the onlookers, wearing a pale yellow suit with a brown spotted bow tie. "What a magnificent marrow! I must congratulate you, Lord Brading."

"Ah, good morning, Dr Delabole," said Dame Barbara pleasantly. "I'm surprised to see you here. I'd have thought you'd be far too busy today to have time for a Flower Show."

Dr Delabole made her an elegant little bow. "On the contrary, Dame Barbara, I wouldn't want to miss *this* Flower Show for anything."

His sister came to stand beside him. She was wearing a large-brimmed white hat and smiling her pale, secret smile. "Lucius is most interested in modern growing methods," she said, "particularly where marrows are concerned."

Suddenly there came a long, moaning sigh, like the wind howling down the chimney on a winter's night.

"It's the marrow!" Susan exclaimed. "I saw it move."

Everyone stared at Lord Brading's marrow. It was rocking gently as though tipped to and fro by an invisible hand.

"The mixture was too strong," said Washington in

a clear, carrying voice. "I knew it would be."

Dr Delabole turned white and his beard quivered dangerously. He took a step towards Washington, clenching his fist. Susan at once moved between them, glaring at him fiercely.

"Be careful, Lucius," warned his sister.

Dame Barbara looked at both of them and at Washington. "What do you mean, the mixture was too strong?" she inquired.

"I saw the formula the other night, when I was taken to his laboratory," Washington explained. "He gave it to the two men who kidnapped me so they could inject it into Lord Brading's marrow and make it bigger than anyone else's."

"Eh? What's that?" Lord Brading's face turned from red to purple. Behind him Gordon tugged at Septimus Sharpe's sleeve and together they began to edge towards the exit.

"Go on, Washington," said Dame Barbara quietly, her eyes fixed on Dr Delabole. "What exactly *did* they inject into the marrow?"

"It was a compound of elephant hormones mixed with one part hydrogen, one part nitrogen, a pinch of sulphur and a teaspoonful of yeast," said Washington.

The marrow gave a violent jerk that brought it to the edge of the table. Susan stared at it in fascination.

"Great heavens!" exclaimed Dame Barbara. "But all that adds up to a highly combustible marrow – nothing less than a potential bomb! Stand well back, everyone. One live spark could set it off!"

Chapter Twenty-Two

The Storm Breaks

The spectators hastily fell back, their eyes riveted to the precariously balanced marrow.

"Absolute nonsense!" Dr Delabole took up a defiant position in front of the table. "The formula is perfectly safe . . ."

At that moment Susan noticed a commotion at the entrance to the marquee where Septimus Sharpe and Gordon, intent on making their escape, had encountered the Misses Trim.

"It's them!" shrieked Miss Evangeline. "The men who attacked Mr Ramage in Mulberry Road – I'd know them anywhere!"

"Know them anywhere!" cried Miss Lavinia, fearlessly grabbing hold of Gordon's coat tail.

Miss Evangeline's eyes fell on Sergeant Fogarty who was close by the entrance, murmuring encouraging words to his gladioli. "Thank heaven – the police!" She pointed an accusing finger at Septimus and Gordon, who were standing rooted to the spot with dismay. "Arrest those two men instantly!"

Sergeant Fogarty looked bewildered. "But I've only just let them go . . ."

Septimus Sharpe decided to take no chances. He seized hold of Gordon's arm and dragged him away from the entrance, which was now blocked by Miss Evangeline and a growing crowd of interested spectators. They dodged behind the display tables and along the back of the tent, seeking a suitable spot to crawl underneath the canvas. Miss Lavinia, still holding on to Gordon's coat, went with them.

Meanwhile Washington had been staring at the marrow. Inside his brain there was a click and a whirr as the RMF came into operation. A slow smile spread over his face. He nudged Susan. "Where can I get some matches?" he asked.

Susan's eyes were fixed on the drama taking place on the other side of the tent. "I don't know," she said vaguely. "Ask Grandad. He may have some."

Washington tugged at Grandad Ramage's sleeve. "Got any matches?" he asked.

Grandad Ramage shook him off impatiently. "Don't carry 'em round any more, not since I gave up me pipe."

At the other end of the tent Miss Evangeline gave Sergeant Fogarty a violent push in the small of his back. "Go on, Sergeant!" she urged furiously. "Are you going to do your duty – or do you intend leaving it all to my sister?"

By now Septimus had succeeded in finding a small gap at the bottom of the canvas. He dropped down on to his stomach, dragging Gordon behind him. "Get a move on!" he hissed. "What's the matter with you?"

"It's this lady," Gordon explained, wiping the perspiration from his forehead. "She won't let me go . . ."

Septimus muttered a few curses and began to wriggle under the canvas.

Washington turned to Lord Brading. "Please, sir, have you any matches?" he inquired.

"What?" Lord Brading stared at him, his mind preoccupied with the extraordinary behaviour of his gamekeeper and footman, to say nothing of the even more extraordinary behaviour of his marrow.

"I need some matches," Washington explained patiently.

Absently Lord Brading fumbled in his pocket and produced a box of Swan Vestas. "Here you are, my lad. Give 'em back when you've done with 'em."

"I will," promised Washington.

Septimus Sharpe, safely through the opening, bent down to pull Gordon after him. Miss Lavinia, seeing her quarry sliding away from her, desperately transferred her grip from Gordon's coat tail to his trouser leg.

"Save my sister!" Miss Evangeline implored, as Miss Lavinia began to disappear beneath the canvas.

Sergeant Fogarty flung himself to the ground, seizing hold of Miss Lavinia's ankles. Miss Evangeline, determined to add her weight to the struggle, resourcefully sat down upon his legs.

Under cover of these dramatic events Washington struck a match and held it carefully against the short stubby stalk of Lord Brading's prize marrow. It took a moment to catch alight, then gradually the flame began to creep along the stalk as if it were the fuse leading to a charge of dynamite. There came a hissing noise, like a slow escape of gas, and a slight crackle as the stalk turned black. For a moment it looked as if the flame might fizzle out, but it flickered alive again, curling round the end of the marrow. The hiss grew louder and the marrow gave a sharp, convulsive twitch. It seemed to swell inside its skin until little cracks appeared, through which a slimy pale green substance began to ooze, bubbling gently. Washington moved hastily away, retreating to a safe position behind Susan.

Suddenly a blinding flash of light filled the tent, followed by a deafening crack which shook the ground and sent everyone diving for cover. Susan threw herself under the nearest trestle table, pulling Washington after her as a shower of wet white flakes sprayed everywhere like sleet, followed by a hailstorm of marrow seeds.

When at last it was over she poked her head through the green baize cover and looked out. The first person she saw was Dr Delabole, who had been standing nearest the marrow when it exploded and was consequently covered from head to foot by the resulting fall-out. Susan began to giggle. "He looks like a pale green melting snowman," she murmured.

Washington lifted the cover to get a better view. "Serve him right," he said unsympathetically.

They scrambled out just as Miss Delabole, who

had been protected from the worst of the downpour by her hat, hurried to her brother's assistance and began to wipe his face with her handkerchief. "Oh, Lucius . . . you're absolutely soaked!"

"It's all *your* fault, Hermione," he snapped, removing a marrow seed from his beard.

Dame Barbara crawled from under a pile of outsize cabbages which had become dislodged during the pandemonium and surveyed the scene. "I'm afraid it was bound to happen, given that particular formula," she said reasonably, extending a helping hand to Grandad Ramage who had been buried beneath the same avalanche. "Perhaps Dr Delabole needs to do a little more work on his researches into modern growing methods . . ."

Dr Delabole shot her a look of acute dislike. "One of these days," he said in a low, menacing voice, "I'll get even with you, Dame Barbara, make no mistake about that."

"Come, Lucius." His sister pulled anxiously at his arm. "I think perhaps we should leave."

As Dame Barbara watched them go she murmured thoughtfully, "On the other hand, I'd have said spontaneous combustion was unlikely . . ."

"Matches!" exclaimed Susan. "Washington asked me for some matches." She looked at him accusingly and he produced the box of matches from behind his back with a grin.

"It must have been the RMF again," groaned Susan. "But who on earth was stupid enough to give them to him?"

Washington handed the matches back to Lord Brading. "Thank you very much, sir," he said politely. "I've finished with them now."

Lord Brading, his hair plastered down over his forehead by the unexpected shower, pocketed the matches and stared disbelievingly at the sad remains of his prize marrow. Only a few tattered pieces of green skin were left on the table. He shook his head wonderingly. "But why . . .?" He appealed to Nat Rumbold. "I don't understand, Nat. Why should anyone do such a thing?"

"Well, my lord, you did promise them extra wages if you won," Nat reminded him.

"So I did." Lord Brading sighed deeply. "Looks like you'll be taking that Cup home again this year after all, Ramage."

Grandad Ramage, who was looking more cheerful than he had for days, agreed that it did seem rather likely.

"They've escaped!" Miss Evangeline Trim, her straw hat askew, came rushing up, following by her sister and a harassed-looking Sergeant Fogarty. "But they won't get far – my sister's made sure of that!"

"Made sure of *that*!" Miss Lavinia echoed, triumphantly waving aloft a pair of grey pin-striped trousers.

"Do you want me to give chase, Arnold?" asked Sergeant Fogarty, who seemed to have developed a slight limp.

Grandad Ramage shook his head. "Let them go," he said generously. "They can't do me any more harm now."

Susan gave him a quick hug. "Congratulations, Grandad! You're going to win . . . I'm certain of it."

Sure enough, the judges came to the unanimous decision that Grandad Ramage's marrow was one of the finest ever seen on Castle Brading village green and he was formally presented with the Cup for yet another year, amidst a storm of applause.

"Well done, Arnold!" Dame Barbara beamed at her brother, putting one arm round Susan's shoulders and the other round Washington's. "In fact, well done everybody! Now I think the least I can do is buy you all an ice-cream."

"I'd rather have a hamburger," said Washington. "And chips."